BITCOIN BEYOND 2140

Its journey to the future of technology

JULES SIMBOLON

Bitcoin beyond 2140 – Its journey to the future of technology

First published in 2024.

Very Finance

Email: Veryfinancial2022@gmail.com

Social Media:

https://www.tiktok.com/@very_finance
https://www.youtube.com/@veryfinance
https://www.instagram.com/very_finance

Paperback ISBN: 9798878886963

Dedicated to my loved ones, who support me.

The Very Finance team and community: thank you for your motivation and inspiration.

Table of Contents

CHAPTER 1:

Introduction to Bitcoin

Since the dawn of civilization, transferring value between distant parties has relied on trusted third-party intermediaries. Central banks issue fiat currencies, while banks and credit card networks facilitate value exchange and maintain ledgers while taking a cut. In 2008, an unknown person or group writing under the pseudonym Satoshi Nakamoto published a whitepaper. The whitepaper described a revolutionary peer-to-peer electronic cash system called Bitcoin.

What is Bitcoin?

Bitcoin is a novel peer-to-peer payment network and cryptocurrency. For the first time, this allowed for the efficient transfer of value over the internet without needing centralized authorities or institutions to verify transactions.

Trust is established cryptographically through mass peer-to-peer collaboration. Records are maintained in a transparent, permanent, decentralised ledger that does not compromise private data.

Bitcoin, fiat money issued by governments and traditional finance differ fundamentally. The Bitcoin network is entirely decentralized, with no central server, hierarchical structure, or authority controlling supply or verification. Worldwide nodes and miners distribute new coins in an autonomous, distributed manner. This contrasts with the monopolistic control central banks have, as they also perform software updates.

Bitcoin's total supply is limited to 21 million bitcoins. It is designed to be gradually released through an automated process called mining over several decades until approximately 2140, when issuance will taper out. This is a key distinction from established currencies with adjustable fiat supplies depending on the issuing authority's monetary policy decisions.

The decentralised Bitcoin ledger has allowed real-time public verification of transactions since its inception. It provides an unprecedented view into how value moves digitally in a highly transparent yet pseudonymous manner. On the other hand, traditional finance settles on private ledgers like SWIFT and relies on intermediaries to dictate terms of transfers shrouded in secrecy.

How Are Bitcoins Created?

The release of new bitcoins into circulation takes place through a decentralized, competitive process known as mining (Nakamoto, 2008). Bitcoin mining involves specialized computers with immense computing capacity working to solve complex cryptographic problems and mathematical puzzles related to each block of transactions (Vranken, 2017). Successfully solving these problems is the mechanism that secures the Bitcoin network and enables the reliable transfer of value without requiring intermediaries (Böhme et al., 2015).

In technical terms, Bitcoin transactions between users are first grouped into candidate blocks. Miners repetitively feed random string numbers through a cryptographic hashing algorithm. This algorithm outputs an essentially unpredictable hash value representing the candidate block (Vranken, 2017). The conditions outlined in the Bitcoin code require this hash value to fall below a dynamically adjusted target threshold that ensures intense difficulty and scarcity (Nakamoto, 2008). Finding a valid solution can involve countless iterations of guessing trillions of random numbers, requiring astronomical processing capacity (Vranken, 2017).

Remarkably, among the global collective of miners, an average of one miner successfully achieves the correct hash every 10 minutes (Nakamoto, 2008). Once found, the winning block is broadcast to the entire Bitcoin network. It is then cryptographically verified and added to the official blockchain, unlocking the mining reward (Vranken, 2017).

Today, a miner's reward consists of newly minted bitcoins and small fees attached to transactions within the confirmed block (Nakamoto, 2008). Originally, in Bitcoin's early history, regular home computers had sufficient power to mine blocks successfully (Vranken, 2017). Competition and difficulty grew exponentially over time in line with Bitcoin's rising adoption (Böhme et al., 2015). As a result, special hardware known as Application-Specific Integrated Circuits (ASICs) became essential to have any realistic chance (Vranken, 2017).

The elaborate mining process introduces new bitcoins in a steady yet gradually slower manner (Nakamoto, 2008). It serves a dual purpose: distributing coins in a founder-free way and independently verifying transactions across the network while resisting tampering by bad-faith actors (Böhme et al., 2015). Together, proof-of-work mining facilitates Bitcoin's groundbreaking capacity as censorship-resistant, decentralised digital money unleashed globally (Vranken, 2017).

How are Bitcoins Stored?

Bitcoin exists solely on its public blockchain ledger, unlike fiat money in bank accounts and centralized databases (Nakamoto, 2008). Instead, what gives individual users actual ownership and control over specific amounts of Bitcoin are private keys (Bonneau et al., 2015).

Bitcoins are associated with addresses, long strings of 26–35 alphanumeric characters. Each address has one public key that is visible openly and a corresponding private key that must be kept secret and safe (Bonneau et al., 2015). Private keys can access, sign transactions with, and move Bitcoin from its associated address to new destinations. These private keys represent control and possession of balance rather than the bitcoins themselves (Nakamoto, 2008).

With this security model, bitcoin storage revolves centrally around ensuring the confidentiality of private keys linked to bitcoin addresses holding balances (Bonneau et al., 2015). There are two main options for users when it comes to wallet solutions for private key management. Users have the option to use external custodial wallets provided by exchanges or third-party providers, which handle security for them. Alternatively, they can choose self-managed non-custodial wallets where users hold their private keys directly (Fleder et al., 2019).

Users can select between software-based desktop and mobile programmes that manage keys digitally or paper-based wallets that print keys for safekeeping (Fleder et al., 2019).

Under all solutions, losing private keys due to destruction, theft, or forgetfulness renders the balance at that address irretrievable. Users must carefully back up and safeguard Bitcoin wallet private keys to protect their money more than with traditional banking (Bonneau et al., 2015). Overall, bitcoins hold financial value only insofar as users possess the underlying private keys that enable control (Nakamoto, 2008). Without access to private keys and their linked secret alphanumeric sequences, the bitcoin residing on the public blockchain remains financially stranded (Fleder et al., 2019).

How do Bitcoin transactions get processed?

The transfer of bitcoin value between addresses, known as a transaction, relies on cryptographic mechanisms that enable secure passage while circumventing issues of trust (Nakamoto, 2008).

Ownership authorization for transmitting bitcoin from one party to another requires leveraging digital signatures associated with the private key of the originating address. This proves to the network that the funds being moved are indeed under the sender's control (Bonneau et al., 2015).

Once a transmission is authorised, the resulting transaction data is broadcast across the peer-to-peer nodes. This data contains crucial metadata, such as the precise amount being sent, timestamp, destination address, and more, and is received by Bitcoin miners (Nakamoto, 2008). To encourage speedy confirmation and discourage fraudulent double spending of already-transmitted bitcoin, transactions have a tiny variable charge, usually under a U.S. dollar (Easley et al., 2019).

Miners incorporate the publicly transmitted Bitcoin transactions into new block candidates. These blocks then undergo the mining validation process, where the next confirmed block in the blockchain is cryptographically chained to prior blocks (Nakamoto, 2008). Once a block containing specific transactions gains about six successive confirmations, it is considered irreversibly set as legitimate by network consensus (Bonneau et al., 2015). Exchanges and merchants that accept Bitcoin normally allow purchases only after a healthy threshold of confirmations to ensure the transaction will remain immutable (Böhme et al., 2015).

This generalised workflow for sending and solidifying transactions using decentralised parties, proof-of-work, and an incentivized confirmation mechanism allows Bitcoin to innovate (Vranken, 2017). Distributing trust in this way enables a seamless peer-to-peer exchange of value. This exchange can occur reliably without the need for identity registration, clearing houses, or jurisdictional authorization (Böhme et al., 2015). Additionally, it operates independently of banks and governments as a self-contained system (Nakamoto, 2008).

The clever incentive structure around Bitcoin transaction fees reinforces miner participation, improving confirmation times and overall network security (Easley et al., 2019). Users can attach fees voluntarily to transaction outputs. During busy and congested periods, they can pay higher fees to prioritise their transfers for faster inclusion by profit-driven miners (Bonneau et al., 2015). The free market dynamic ensures an economic drive among miners. They act as the distributed honest custodians of Bitcoin's immutable ledger, confirming transactions (Vranken, 2017).

Focusing on transaction processing throughput and minimising confirmation times led to new scaling solutions built next to base-layer Bitcoin (Croman et al., 2016). The Lightning Network represents a Layer 2 improvement that settles net positions in Bitcoin's base layer to offer limitless transactional bandwidth (Poon & Dryja, 2016). Lightning harnesses the security assurances of the underlying blockchain to enable instant, low-cost cryptocurrency transactions (Rohrer et al., 2019). These transactions are ideal for point-of-sale usage at register checkouts and leverage the immutable decentralisation attributes of the base blockchain (Fleder et al., 2019).

Bitcoin operates as a reliable and secure monetary base layer, thanks to segregated scaling solutions and modular architecture (Croman et al., 2016). These preserve its revolutionary attributes of immutability and censorship resistance without compromise (Böhme et al., 2015). Meanwhile, complementary modules purpose-built for transactional efficiency or dApp composability fulfill more progressive functions atop bedrock foundations (Vranken, 2017). This concurrent advancement across verticals reinforces Bitcoin's versatility and scope (Bonneau et al., 2015).

Decentralized Development

A major source of Bitcoin's market value and resiliency against corruption is its decentralized open-source development culture around technical governance. No entity, developer team, or government body controls the Bitcoin network, unlike traditional finance and large tech (Böhme et al., 2015). Maintenance is decentralized, driven by consensus and peer review, rather than controlled by corporate hierarchies or political influence (Vranken, 2017).

Bitcoin's decentralised ethos remains faithful to its origins as "cash with wings" powered by blockchain technology. It carries forward the momentum created by Satoshi Nakamoto while also resisting the consolidation of control by centralised entities (Nakamoto, 2008). Cutting-edge cryptocurrency technology flourishes thanks to its modular architecture, decentralised team structures, and rough consensus model (Croman et al., 2016). It is built upon the proven and immutable Bitcoin protocol, providing a solid bedrock foundation (Böhme et al., 2015).

Bitcoin's underlying consensus mechanism and rule set are firmly solidified. However, software-based innovation continues to improve functional capacity without compromising security fundamentals at ancillary layers (Vranken, 2017). Open-source developers worldwide are building complementary technologies.

Lightning Network, a supplementary layer, enables extremely scalable Bitcoin transactions and complex smart contract capability (Poon & Dryja, 2016). Bitcoin can continue evolving without excessively tweaking its battle-tested base layer protocol using a layered modular architecture approach (Croman et al., 2016).

Bitcoin's decentralised ethos remains faithful to its origins as "cash with wings," enabled by blockchain technology. It carries forward the momentum created by Satoshi Nakamoto and opposes the concentration of control in centralised entities (Nakamoto, 2008). Cutting-edge cryptocurrency technology flourishes thanks to the modular stacks of software, decentralised team structures, and rough consensus model (Croman et al., 2016). This is built upon a solid bedrock foundation of the proven and immutable Bitcoin protocol (Böhme et al., 2015).

Innovations can happen much faster at the upper layers using a layered technology stack a decentralizedised team structure (Croman et al., 2016). Changes to the base consensus protocol, on the other hand, undergo extensive peer review and testing. The modular architecture reinforces Bitcoin's assurances around security at a massive scale (Vranken, 2017). It achieves this through layers of abstraction, distilling separately from the task of expanding functionality to adjacent constructs purpose-built for specific applications (Croman et al., 2016).

Segregated development workstreams also allow the compartmentalization of duties. Protocol custodians strictly focus on preserving Bitcoin's decentralization attributes and censorship-resistance properties that uphold its apolitical neutrality (Böhme et al., 2015). Complementary modules like Lightning Network handle tasks around embeddability into consumer apps, requiring separate design considerations (Poon & Dryja, 2016). This division of tasks allows professionals in protocol development, cryptography, and user-centered design to focus on their strengths (Croman et al., 2016).

The Birth of Bitcoin's Revolution

Crypto-anarchists and cypherpunks saw it coming, but the first stable foundation for digital cash and decentralised currency didn't exist until 2008. A whitepaper titled "Bitcoin: A Peer-to-Peer Electronic Cash System" was published on a cryptography mailing list on October 31st, 2008. Someone using the pseudonym Satoshi Nakamoto wrote the paper.

The text described a solution that cleverly combined proof-of-work and a data structure called the blockchain. This solution effectively addressed the difficult problem of preventing double spending without relying on trusted third parties.

This whitepaper did not materialize spontaneously without a preceding ideological foundation. For decades, libertarian activists had foreseen the possibility of mathematically secured digital money divorced from state monopolies and censorship. Cypherpunk thought leaders Timothy May and Nick Szabo extensively wrote about the game theory of securing value transfer via technology alone in the 1990s. Nakamoto later made use of their intellectual foundation.

Concurrently, foundational advances in cryptography like b-money, Hashcash, and BitGold pioneered concepts core to Bitcoin, including mining via proof-of-work as a Sybil resistance mechanism.

How it All Started: The Cypherpunk Quest for Digital Cash

An obscure tribe of radicals across academia, activism, and the tech industry nurtured visions of an anonymous digital cash system for decades. Uncrackable cryptography would protect this system. This motley band of cypherpunks yearned to build stateless money as a catalyst for preserving financial privacy against creeping authoritarian surveillance (Hughes, 1993).

In 1992, Intel engineer Timothy May circulated The Crypto Anarchist Manifesto among fellow travellers gathered in California. This marked the beginning of their ambitious crusade. May's treatise glowingly anticipated cryptography so impenetrably secure that it facilitates anonymous interactions online (May, 1992). But commerce requires an exchange of value.

In order to address these challenges, it was necessary to create a form of digital cash that replicated important monetary characteristics, particularly verifiable scarcity. Digital cash had to

9

outperform gold, which lost its global dominance due to central bankers' erratic behaviour in the 20th century (Friedman & Schwartz, 1963). It also needed to be resistant to coercive seizures.

Computer scientist David Chaum's early 1980s cryptography, eCash, failed due to its reliance on a centralised mint binding system (Chaum, 1983). Chaum discovered the risks of dependence on single issuing authorities when his eCash startup, DigiCash, declared bankruptcy in 1998 (Froomkin, 1996). This termination resulted in the failure of the pioneering but closed-loop network that supported tokens spent like physical banknotes.

Cypherpunk ideologues learned painful lessons that reinforced their convictions. They believed that only decentralised open networks with no systemic chokepoints could sustain censorship-resistant peer-to-peer money, insulating identity and preserving sovereignty (Hughes, 1993). Pioneers like Timothy May and Nick Szabo explored means for ungoverned transactions, shaking off state shackles and banking the unbanked beyond oligarchic manipulations (Szabo, 1998).

Szabo built on the work of Wei Dai, a computing engineer. In 1998, Dai outlined the theoretical concept of "b-money" constructed on distributed ledgers. In this system, network participants vouchsafe balances separately to increase resilience against individual coercion. But unreliability challenges around ensuring continual connectivity and tamper-proof messaging remained daunting.

Cryptographer Nick Szabo advanced concepts for "bit gold" money minted through computerized puzzle solving to concentrate digital scarcity without central oversight (Szabo, 2005). Still, obstacles around reliably tracking coin ownership and preventing fabrication risks through hacking stymied implementations during the 1990s.

The gulf between bloated banking bureaucracy and the efficiency revolutionising communications and creativity across once disparate internet tribes was escalating (Castells, 2000). However, cypherpunk science still frustratingly eluded the realisation of digital cash without a custodian as the 21st century approached. Then in 2008, an obscure whitepaper appeared from an unknown person or group pseudonymously called Satoshi Nakamoto, unveiling one word that changed everything: bitcoin. Visionary architecture fused preceding fragments into a unified firmware indelibly etched into history's arc towards emancipation and optionality.

Nakamoto assimilated concepts like British cryptographer Adam Back's proof-of-work demonstrating energy expenditure without relying on human vouching vulnerable by self-interest (Back, 2002). Coin minting is bound by a quantifiable computing cost, verified instantly, and impossible to falsify at scale. Peer participation in a public transaction ledger increases probabilistic security magnitudes due to brute brain and number crunching force, eliminating Sybil vulnerabilities.

Nakamoto fulfilled his manifest destiny by debuting an anonymous email list. This culminated in a genesis block etched for posterity. They escaped cypherpunks repeatedly, just shy of the secured shoreline. Bitcoin's launch broke down legacy barriers and established itself as a credible cryptocurrency with superior capabilities (Böhme et al., 2015).

However, it still has inferior trust compared to its established counterparts, which are burdened by moral hazard and misaligned governance (Friedman & Schwartz, 1963).

Publishing the Whitepaper: A Novel Digital Currency

Nakamoto masterfully synthesized these threads when he released version 0.1 of the Bitcoin software three months after the initial cryptographic mailing list debut. The open-source Bitcoin code was launched on SourceForge on January 3rd, 2009.

This initiated the Bitcoin network by mining the first ever block, known as the genesis block. The genesis block conveyed a timely message about Bitcoin's necessity as a censorship-proof alternative to incumbent finance. It was engraved with a Times headline about bank bailouts.

First Years of Bitcoin: Pizza Purchases and Early Adoption

In 2010, Laszlo Hanyecz, an early Bitcoin contributor, made the first recorded human transaction. He paid 10,000 bitcoins to get a pair of Papa John's pizzas, which were valued at approximately $30 (Brito & Castillo, 2013).

This ordinary meal purchase was seen as frivolous spending at the time. However, it became immortalised as the first material item ever directly exchanged for digital currency (Nian & Chuen, 2015). This marked Bitcoin's first step towards becoming a medium of exchange rather than just a speculative bet.

During the initial years, usage of the network was mainly by cryptography enthusiasts and libertarians. They were attracted to both the technical merits and political leanings of a permissionless financial network that had no authority to answer to (Böhme et al., 2015). Bitcoin cultivated an increasingly diverse early adopter base over the subsequent months. This was driven by ideological convictions and the prospects of exponential returns as innovative digital money (Gandal & Halaburda, 2014).

All the while, Bitcoin operated outside the mainstream purview until October 2011, when a Gawker article directed a flood of popular attention (Chen, 2011). This enchanted the public with this bizarre electronic currency being used to buy everything from pizza to narcotics on purpose-built anonymous marketplaces.

Identifying Satoshi Nakamoto: Linguistic and Spatial Clues

But the most enduring intrigue has concerned the origins of Bitcoin itself and the true identity of its founder, Satoshi Nakamoto. This specter-like figure communicated sporadically before vanishing when his creation was still nascent. By giving Bitcoin life pseudonymously, Nakamoto deliberately shrouded its provenance in the secrecy that persists today.

Many have attempted to deduce Nakamoto's identity based on limited evidence such as whitepaper metadata, writing style, and forum history. These sources offer intriguing but inconclusive insights into their occupation and political beliefs (Wright & Filippi, 2015). Linguistics analysis narrows Nakamoto's native language down to English in the British Isles as the most probable option (Juola, 2013). Furthermore, blockchain timestamp analysis traces sleep cycles to predominantly Japanese and North American time zones (Kaminska, 2011). Both geographies have prime suspects. One of them is cryptocurrency pioneer Nick Szabo (Popper, 2015). He penned foundational scholarship around digital money conceptual precursors to Bitcoin and denies that he is Nakamoto.

Other conjectured candidates include cryptography legend Hal Finney, who received Nakamoto's first Bitcoin test transaction (Greenberg, 2014). Finney lived close to a resident who closely resembled police sketches of Nakamoto. The sketches were derived from interactions with cryptocurrency company staff that Nakamoto corresponded extensively with (Wallace, 2011). However, no smoking gun ever definitively surfaced, confirming any individual's identity and allowing the mythos of Nakamoto to balloon unencumbered.

Disappearance of Nakamoto: Passing the Torch

By December 2010, over a year after Bitcoin v0.1 was released, Nakamoto correspondence patterns showed declining engagement with the community. After distributing the software and stabilising the network, Nakamoto stepped back and handed control to Gavin Andresen. This marked a transitional moment for Bitcoin's governance as Andresen gained enhanced administrative privileges over code repositories (Vigna & Casey, 2015). Finally, on April 26, 2011, after freezing forum activity for months, Nakamoto signed off with a farewell email to collaborators:

"I've moved on to other things. It's in good hands with Gavin and everyone." (Vigna & Casey, 2015)

Bitcoin's iconic founder permanently receded from direct involvement, capping an improbable chapter of the anonymous contribution that birthed a technical tour de force. Nakamoto went quiet, and the cryptocurrency continued to grow beyond imagination year after year.

Legacy of Nakamoto: Inspiring Innovation Unbound

The intense debate around Nakamoto's disappearing act sparked theories. These theories ranged from cashing out bitcoin wealth early on to intelligence agency origins (Böhme et al., 2015). There are even speculations that Nakamoto is deceased (Wile, 2014).

The most likely explanation, echoing Nakamoto's parting words, is that a creator was satisfied with the fulfilment of their vision for kickstarting decentralised digital money (Nakamoto, 2008). However, without absolute confirmation, this remains uncertain. Therefore, it was time to let Bitcoin stand on its own, unaffected by any centralized authority.

Bitcoin realises much more integrity as a politically neutral platform resilient against influence. It cements ethically sound money principles without identity baggage and direct figureheads that can be coerced (Böhme et al., 2015). Bitcoin has thrived without its chief architect, remaining true to its name—fatherless, motherless, and genealogically unbound from conventional paradigms. Yet, it passionately tends to the needs of a growing flock each year.

Today, Nakamoto's legacy persists through the ever-expanding echo of that original whitepaper shared widely online, now translated into dozens of languages. Bitcoin's committed technical stewardship has inspired echoes that ripple onward, fueling an entire industry of next-generation blockchain innovation. This includes Ethereum's smart contract revolution and the expanding Web3 ecosystem (Vigna & Casey, 2015).

The re-emergence of Nakamoto to prove any single identity theory right may lead to enlightenment, as it would make us realise how many Nakamotos now walk among us. They are the decentralised keepers. The vision was kindled anonymously over a decade ago. When one sees the true scale of Bitcoin, narrowness becomes insignificant. It is a living testament constantly upgraded and fortified by conventional energy, surpassing any individual's efforts (Böhme et al., 2015).

Why Was Bitcoin Created?

Modern banking and money trace their origins to goldsmiths, who pioneered the storage and transfer of value between market participants. Goldsmiths became crucial financial intermediaries by confiscating gold and issuing paper banknotes representing ownership. This centralized management of money enabled wider transferability beyond physical exchange.

However, it also concentrated tremendous power in entities entrusted with guaranteeing redemption rights over national savings.

These entities also received custody fees and privileges, like fractional reserve lending against deposits.

Over the past two centuries, fractional reserve banking has matured into a sprawling industry, imprinting irreversible complexity into the financial system. Major banks and quasi-governmental central banks are responsible for influencing monetary policy and the supply of money circulating in the economy. They form a tight mesh, building on economies of scale.

Central banks exert tremendous command over inflation, credit cycles, and macroeconomic trajectories by creating money and manipulating interest rates. The Federal Reserve was created in 1913 with the mandate to ensure price stability and address high unemployment and inflation. However, its monetary actions over the years indicate a significant shift in focus and a tendency towards short-term thinking. The Federal Reserve's policies frequently contribute to the business cycles they aim to manage.

This is because they tend to overstimulate economies with cheap debt, leading to painful corrections when inflation necessitates sudden policy adjustments. Theoretical assumptions around using fiscal and monetary stimulus to smooth markets were thus debunked in reality over subsequent decades marked by endemic financialization.

Cypherpunk Philosophy

An obscure group of thinkers began congregating online in the early 1990s. The individuals identified themselves as cypherpunks. They were focused on utilizing cryptography for social and political change in response to deepening distrust in centralized institutions (Hughes, 1993). The diverse group consisted of libertarian anarchists, engineers, and computer scientists. They questioned status quo governance across information security, digital privacy, and financial autonomy in a radical manner.

Thought leaders such as Eric Hughes, Timothy May, and Nick Szabo have explored decentralised alternatives to societal trust intermediaries (Hughes, 1993). These alternatives range from assurance authorities issuing digital certificates to the extensive control that banks have over the financial ledger. The cypherpunk movement anticipated the emergence of a natively digital currency because of its shared mistrust of authoritative gatekeepers (Szabo, 2005). This currency would serve as a tool for individuals to transfer untraceable value to any state entity while being susceptible to security flaws, coercive influence, and corruption.

Szabo wrote extensively about the game theory dynamics for secure digital money infrastructure independent of sovereign policy risk (Szabo, 2005). The proto-Bitcoin theories conceptualised "bit gold" models. These models relied on cryptographic proof instead of trust in third-party vaults to independently verify the integrity of transactions. Combining self-executing "smart contracts" with digital scarcity pinned to mathematical proofs, cypherpunk visionaries laid ideological foundations for Bitcoin's eventual catalysis (Szabo, 2005).

Specific Failures Motivating Bitcoin's Creation

The late 2000s brewed a noxious cocktail of foundational cracks across system-wide pillars inappropriately propped up by duct tape and dental floss for decades. The subprime mortgage crisis caused major financial institutions to suffer. They had been making money while ignoring the rising systemic risk that arose from flawed risk management models.

The insolvency crisis quickly spiralled uncontrollably. Drastic interventions like unprecedented Wall Street bailouts aroused an intensifying ire regarding the tangled proximity between regulators and the institutions being regulated.

Further infuriating technologists, WikiLeak's publication of leaked confidential materials shed sunlight on military misconduct yet also provoked thundering backlash from incumbents. Under intense political pressure, payment processors and banks erected financial blockades against the whistleblower non-profit. This cut off access to citizen donations and suffocated revenue streams.

Cypherpunks witnessed censorship weaponization directly sabotaging digital commerce. This made clear the pressing need for state-agnostic money beyond oligarchic reach. This need was emphasised by such brazen demonstrations of financial coercion.

Satoshi Nakamoto published the Bitcoin whitepaper in 2008. The whitepaper introduced decentralised digital money, aiming to empower individuals and reduce reliance on paternalistic institutions. Nakamoto achieved the cypherpunk dream of direct financial freedom by establishing verifiable transaction finality without intermediaries. This system is protected from coercive pressures that affect traditional money.

Bitcoin's Potential Impact on Traditional Finance: Undermining Monetary Sovereignty

The monetary monopoly that nation-states have held for centuries is under threat thanks to the introduction of Bitcoin. Central banks exercised essentially dictatorial control over the currency supplies underlying national economies. Throughout history, unchecked inflationary policies have repeatedly undermined public purchasing power to dangerous extremes, eroding livelihoods and fermenting dissent. Those savings held hostage to political whims perpetually now possess an alternative home to take refuge in, dramatically disrupting antiquated monopolies over money itself.

By introducing a mathematical scarcity cap of 21 million units, Bitcoin weaves sound money attributes into purely digital form for the first time. Unlike infinitely printable fiat, subject to unbounded manipulation, bitcoins enter circulation gradually and verifiably through decentralized minting. "Digital gold" emerges as a multi-trillion-dollar parallel financial system. It balances sovereign monetary regimes and provides an escape valve for citizens poorly served by hyper-indebted governments pursuing short-term enrichment over long-term stability.

Pioneering institutional investors like hedge funds, university endowments, and corporations now hold bitcoin on balance sheets as treasury reserve assets. This is because bitcoin is uncorrelated with traditional stock and bond markets, foreshadowing its inevitability. Bitcoin was initially seen as play money for computer nerds. However, early innovative adopters recognised the potential for significant upside exposure at modest portfolio weights due to Bitcoin's attractive risk/reward probability.

Latecomers face significant opportunity costs for delaying meaningful investigation, as their gambit proved wise beyond imagination. The addressable market limits the price discovery for non-sovereign digital gold. This market expands as mainstream recognition of Bitcoin's utility and monetary properties grows.

Central bankers are accustomed to acting boldly against savers. They are now facing a harsh reality. More and more global citizens choose to seek refuge in uncensorable cryptocurrencies that are resistant to inflationary debasement. Attempts to restrict usage directly trigger Streisand effects, drawing a regulatory spotlight that brings more attention and familiarity with once obscure monetary alternatives. This cascades into a self-reinforcing vortex steadily draining power from institutions historically enjoying money monopoly positions.

The loss of monetary primacy follows the sudden emergence of independent parallel rails carrying value securely without institutional assistance previously deemed indispensable. Media gatekeepers failed to adapt business models to internet distribution.

Central bankers stare into the abyss of disintermediation as trusted financial custodians upon which entire economies have relied for centuries.

The exponentially growing flock chooses to secure and transact value directly on cryptocurrency protocols. They also choose to consume and share content directly on social platforms. This effectively dashes hopes for resuming bygone levels of relevance, revenue, and importance moving forward.

Evolution of Money

Expanding from its first principles as apolitical, decentralized money, Bitcoin continues maturing as tempered digital gold optimized for perseverance and security. Successive technological generations build adjacent value layers atop Bitcoin foundations. These layers incorporate expanded functionality around lending, derivatives, and automated contracts customized for wider needs.

Bitcoin remains the supreme monetary energy reservoir. It underwrites those ancillary experiments, much like kinetic gold historically gave rise to fractional paper receipts. This emerging symbiosis between an ultimate anchor and protocol suite supports broader maturity.

Through its short life, Bitcoin has developed network effects that resemble the enduring nature of widely used standards like IP or TCP/IP, which gain more stability over time. Bitcoin's potential irrelevance is often overlooked due to its strong path dependence. Additionally, the high costs associated with reversing the momentum of an entire parallel financial system contribute to this oversight.

Bitcoin's technological lead and high replacement cost offer competitive advantages as more users join in the coming years. It would be practically implausible for nation-states to intervene violently and coordinately due to the globally distributed computation and capital. Critics failed to grasp early on that money forms an energy-like infrastructure system. It is imperative to understand this today, as it underpins entire economies.

Similar to other foundational platforms like telecommunications or transportation grids, money exhibits entrenched network effects over time. The more participants rely on universally accepted currencies, the more reinforcement builds, further cementing dominance. Utilizing these dynamics first in the novel world of natively digital money that visionary cryptography has unlocked has led to Bitcoin's ascent.

The disruptive currency, born on the internet, has succeeded the US dollar as a global reserve asset backing world trade today. Real-world faith strengthens it. It follows the same path as the dollar when it succeeds gold holdings. Bitcoin's infrastructural nature imparts Lindy qualities to the underlying money itself. This makes it more unassailable over each rising cycle and consolidates value anchored on profoundly secure technological foundations.

Far from facing decline, Bitcoin's versatile extensibility supports sustained relevance and increasing criticality thanks to enabling modular innovation atop stable base layers. Bitcoin ensures scarcity and guarantees a final settlement. Exponential development occurs in the technology stack.

Lightning-fast payments, sophisticated smart contract functionality, and front-end experiences integrate cryptocurrency's advantages into simpler applications for the benefit of end users. This development has been observed. This concurrent specialization into complementary capability planes reinforces technological leadership in all verticals.

Path Towards Mainstream Adoption

The challenges of using cryptocurrency have significantly improved since its inception. They will continue to do so as the layered infrastructure becomes more solid. The early years were characterized by a lot of speculation and volatility as well as initial confusion over the departure from conventional money. However, genuine progress in technology, finance, and education has alleviated most of these hurdles, leading to greater public preparedness for this disruptive entrant.

Reputable companies, such as traditional exchanges, are introducing consumer-friendly models on technological fronts. These models allow users to hold Bitcoin indirectly without bearing sole custody through custodial services. This shifts the burden of education or securing keys onto regulated financial entities already providing conventional interfaces to legacy money management.

The impatience with Bitcoin's approximately 3 transactions per second speed also led to the development of innovative Layer 2 solutions, such as the Lightning Network. This network effectively creates limitless transactional bandwidth while utilising the security assurances of the underlying blockchain. By settling net positions at Bitcoin's base layer, Lightning enables instant, low-cost cryptocurrency transactions ideal for point-of-sale usage at register checkouts.

On financial fronts, greater awareness of Bitcoin's favorable risk-adjusted return indicators like the Sharpe Ratio empowers prudent probability-based allocation decisions by large institutions. The snowball effect draws in corporate treasuries, pension funds, sovereign wealth funds, and eventually retail mutual funds and ETFs. This amplifies positive momentum by enlarging intermediation pipelines.

Progress on these multiple fronts is key to lowering barriers to mainstream adoption by the wider public across technology and finance. Bitcoin already enjoys first-mover momentum internationally, exhibiting "Lindy" antifragile attributes as its network size and value grow. The surrounding ecosystem continues to mature, concurrent with a broader understanding by users and governments are still gaining familiarity when structuring policy responses.

The increasing public familiarity comes alongside the proliferation of tools and services from industry startups. These tools and services are explicitly designed to provide smoother onboarding into Bitcoin's decentralised financial fabric for newcomers. Convenient mobile applications enable buying cryptocurrency via debit cards and managing holdings alongside traditional assets. Contrast that with the early pioneer era, which was characterized by significant usability issues.

These ventures improve education by highlighting important aspects such as self-custody, private keys, and permissionless access. They fulfil Bitcoin's promise of direct financial sovereignty without intermediaries historically prone to rent extraction. User experience refinements incrementally invite wider participation at scale into decentralized money's profound advantages.

CHAPTER 2:

Bitcoin as an Investment

Before analyzing Bitcoin's investment prospects, exploring what constitutes "good money" and why sound monetary properties matter tremendously is imperative. Blockchain technology is changing assumptions about the structure of money. It is revealing limitations that have hindered progress for centuries in the roles played by printed paper or metal discs valued based on shared hallucinations.

Return now to the first principles around the evolving phenomenon of money itself. Consider its progressive features across eras, alongside periodic interruptions repressing potential. This foundation is best equipped to chart Bitcoin's trajectory as an apex of monetary innovation and is perfectly fit for digitally native internet citizens.

Defining Key Monetary Properties

Well-functioning money aims to reliably fulfill three primary roles within an economy: storing value by maintaining predictable purchasing power over long timeframes. Serving as an accepted medium of exchange to facilitate trade by representing generalized value, allowing specialization beyond inconvenient barter dependencies. And providing a standard uniform unit of account allowing price assignment to goods or services as reference benchmarks simplified by numerical designations that all counterparties universally accept.

Several key properties contribute towards stability and retention across these monetary functions. The durability of the monetary substance must persist intact through continuous handling and exchange without deterioration. Portability is essential for convenient transferability by physical persons or transmission mechanisms. Appropriate divisibility into smaller, fungible units enables sufficient price granularity across transaction contexts.

Uniformity in measurable quality or design offers reassurance against weighing, assessing, or validating each monetary unit upon exchange. And crucially, a reliably capped supply resists boundless inflationary dilution that severely disrupts economic signaling and planning when uncontrolled political pressures prevail.

Over millennia of civilization, various physical substances have emerged as informal money due to possessing desirable qualities before top-down formalization by rulers. Decorative seashells, textile fabrics, brightly colored cinnabar minerals, and feather quills served as early stores of value and means of trade in the absence of centralized state currencies. Ancient China has also used compressed tea cubes as monetary units since the Tang Dynasty.

The universal attributive value of precious metals like gold and silver for ornamental applications ultimately led to their dominant monetary status. This was due to their natural scarcity and alluring aesthetic luster. The commodities facilitated exchange in the absence of numeric designations, abstract financial ledgers, or third-party issuance authorities. They served as the closest early approximation to ideal monetary properties, ensuring that relying users were not betrayed or faced with illegitimate claims.

Gold and silver coins circulated in societies where metallism prevailed. These coins contained intrinsic precious metal content, serving as the source of value itself rather than relying on representational claims that could be debased if sovereign backing failed. Physical commodities served as the evidentiary basis for value, rather than fragile promises that required trust in the credibility of centralized issuing institutions.

Fiat national currencies introduced unprecedented governmental discretion over inflationary money printing. These currencies are now detached from reserves backed by gold or silver, which previously anchored currency legitimacy for centuries. This conferred extravagant advantages, enabling sovereign deficit spending at the long-term expense of savers and economic stability.

Political restraint and tenuous public trust are the only factors that prevent national bankers from engaging in unrestrained base money expansion. They seek to fund state growth or incentivize economic output beyond justifiable levels matched to organic productivity. Central banks still face the rhetorical and policy conundrum of preserving buying power stability, issuing unbacked money, and controlling economic cycles.

Wallet-ready state currencies have versatile utility, allowing for efficient deployment of monetary tools. However, fiat systems come with overwhelming complexity, unpredictability, and moral hazard compared to intrinsically-backed commodity money that requires no trust in human discretion. Those in power often break their promises to maintain currency stability due to the temptation of pursuing self-interested inflationary policies. These policies have delayed consequences and allow them to avoid immediate blame.

A historical tension in making sure stable monetary properties is finding a balance between the temporary usefulness of fiat currency and the value loss of commodity currency models. Today, the tug-of-war between government-backed bank money and emergent cryptocurrency rivals like Bitcoin reflects the centralization versus decentralization theme. They strive to enhance standards through consensus-secured software.

Early Evolutionary Stages of Money

Decentralized bartering systems allowed for the earliest forms of value exchange between goods and services long before there were formal currencies. These systems did not require the use of intermediate instruments such as coins or paper bills that represent abstract generalized purchasing power (Graeber, 2011). Unreliability in locating reciprocal bartering partners wanting complementary items hindered transaction volumes. When low supply/demand probabilities did not catalyze exchanges, this constraint limited specialization prospects to subsistence farming or craftsmanship.

The gradual loosening of strict conventions surrounding early pseudo-monetary commodities such as salt, tea leaves, feathers, or decorative jewelry or items allowed for indirect exchange and profit motivations (Einzig 1966). These goods didn't officially constitute defined money yet but circulated similarly as a tradable store of value and exchange medium. Wampum served as ritual gift currency among North American tribes, conveying meanings beyond face utility. Durable substantive items slowly assumed more transactional roles over time, given their universal appreciation. These provided a bridge, helping match counterparts across proximity and needs—something lacking in primitive bartering.

The emergence of commodities as primitive bearer certificates contributed to smoothing trade. It also unlocked economic specialization beyond agriculture and skilled craftsmanship, no longer constrained by the deficiencies of direct bartering. Population centers arose as marketplaces matching varied counterparts expanded. Before state-minted money centuries later, early civilizations traded seashells, beads, tea bricks, and silk bolts as culturally desirable items.

In 1500 BC, ancient Egypt first utilized gold and silver rings as a medium of exchange, foreshadowing the original electrum gold coins later minted in Lydia, controlled by King Alyattes. His heir, King Croesus, later advanced bi-metallic coinage by issuing pure silver and gold pieces stamped with the lion head motif as a royal guarantor of quality and weight (Bernstein 2000). These provided immense advantages over crude barter by enabling the indirect exchange of third-party-issued monetary instruments possessing intrinsic commodity value. Their portability conferred efficiencies against hauling clumsy inventory for direct trade.

Transportable metal coins derive their value from controlled ratios of gold and silver content. These coins slowly disseminated across advancing empires, offering convenience and verifiability advantages to those eager to adopt this monetary innovation. Large amounts of coins with regional authority images could be struck to efficiently collect taxes and issue army pay, fueling conquering ambitions. The fungibility of currency also benefited the reliability and administration of sprawling domains versus variable livestock or grains vulnerable to situational devaluations.

The twin stimuli of ease for rulers and alleviation of trade inconveniences commoditized coinage. This saw meteoric support, greatly accelerating monetary utility into an indispensable pillar of increasingly sophisticated civilizations. Coin advances improved prosperity and specialization, while democratized marketplace access accelerated economic growth beyond millennia of primitive trading and painful commodity money. These changes in social coordination efficiency still benefit modernity.

Modern cryptocurrency seeks to uphold economic assurance and independence by technologically enforcing algorithmic reliability, where only political promises persuade. Early gold and electrum coinage set enduring expectations for sound, reliable money that empowers individuals rather than subjugates them to instability and confusion.

Money in Ancient Civilizations

Metallurgy mastery progressed in ancient civilizations. This led to a transition in the value of precious metals like gold and silver from decorative purposes to trusted forms of exchangeable value between people (Bernstein, 2000). The inherent scarcity and unique properties of gold and silver made them ideal as monetary instruments that could circulate across tribes. Stamped coins became a widely trusted currency.

Metal coinage enabled early economies of scale in agrarian cultures, with merchants and bankers beyond farmers (Davies, 2002). These specialisations raised overall living standards and drove a higher demand for money compared to simple bartering systems. Flying currency was established in ninth-century China under the Tang Dynasty as a supplement to bronze coins and silver ingots (Goetzmann & Rouwenhorst, 2005).

These paper banknotes were partially redeemable against the metal currencies. By providing a paper alternative, metal transportation burdens were greatly reduced across the large territory of the empire. Skepticism about over-issuance not backed by metallic reserves periodically created hyperinflations that destabilized the kingdom in its closing centuries (Goetzmann & Rouwenhorst, 2005). These early monetary science lessons showcase the fine line that fiat money systems must tread between convenience, flexibility, stability, and confidence. Excessive unbacked printing for short-term ends risks jeopardizing faith in the entire monetary regime over the long run.

Paper notes gained popularity in Asia between the 9th and 15th centuries. Meanwhile, metallic forms of money continued to evolve in medieval Europe, despite temporary setbacks during the Dark Ages after the fall of Rome. By the early 13th century, Florence's gold florin coin was the Mediterranean's major trading currency (Spufford, 1988), making it Europe's banking center.

Florin's reliability boosted cross-border trade and financial dealings.

In Africa, East African traders relied on stamped seashells and beads as a trusted money medium along the Indian Ocean maritime trade routes. This reliance was cemented through extensive trading (Hogendorn & Johnson, 1986). These standardized shells efficiently facilitated growing commercial exchanges across the eastern coast of the continent.

The unique, native shells held intrinsic collectible value while also serving proto-monetary functions of exchange before the colonial age. Their organic durability and portability proved more convenient than bartering mismatched goods in coastal swaps. Just as Florida connected prosperity in Europe, these stamped shells connected lands across the Indian Ocean trade zone. In West Africa, beads imported through North African trade similarly served as money for inland exchanges during medieval times.

Money in the Middle Ages

While ancient civilizations progressed in their monetary systems and usage, European feudalism repressed economic growth from the 9th to the 15th centuries (Spufford, 1988). After the fall of the western Roman Empire, limited rural manorial barter exchanges dominated basic economic transactions in this dark age. These exchanges extended from feudal manor estates to village markets. These involved the awkward exchange of impractical goods like grains, textiles, animals, etc. that plagued inconsistencies and complicated trade over even short distances.

However, by the 11th century, the first glimmers of financial sophistication defiant to the bartering status quo emerged from growing Italian city-states like Florence. The gold florin, minted in 1252 (Spufford, 1988), quickly became the main currency for facilitating major commerce across the Mediterranean trading world. It worked in partnership with the silver ducat of Venice.

The florin, backed by the city's rising banking houses and supply lines linked to gold from North African mines, epitomized monetary reliability during the era of the crusades. It also became known for its portability in long-distance luxury trades. These new proto-global currencies fueled the early economic dominance of significant Italian city-state republics.

These city-states had the regional metallurgical and financial competencies necessary to provide currencies central to opening trade barriers with Arab and Middle Eastern partners. Thereby, they could furnish the coins most in pan-European demand while fueling their own family ruling houses, like the Medicis. Historian Peter Spufford analyzed in 1988 that the florin and ducat demonstrated early centralization of bullion and significant commercial finance in regions like Tuscany and Venice. Meanwhile, feudal rural barter remained stagnant for centuries.

By enabling rising merchant class labor mobility and supporting it with concrete financial incentives, these urban currencies weakened the foundations of previous closed fiefdom systems. Glimmers of monetary momentum hinted at what could become possible with economies open beyond subsistent containment under baron estates.

The discovery of Aztec and Incan bullion troves in the Americas in the early 1500s led to dramatic expansions of the European money supply and minting scales. This occurred as nation-states like Spain centralized mining claims and colonial plunder extraction.

The enormous silver influx provided ample new coinage reserves. This enabled the continent's ensuing commercial banking systems to sprout and thrive upon fractional reserve storage lending dynamics. Opportunists maximized paper note issuances against silver in vaults, releasing wider credit access while limiting risk exposure through shrewd leverage ratios. This allowed them to turn the stolen precious metals to their advantage (Quinn, 2001).

Thereby, shadier colonial strengthening expanded monetary possibilities at home. It kicked off exponential business financing capabilities for the merchant class. This allowed them to dramatically extend trade and production scales, backed by credit amplification vehicles developed in institutions like the Bank of Amsterdam by 1609.

During the Song Dynasty in China, alongside the globalization of bullion, paper money also continued to evolve. It became the first known government-issued note to be legal tender in 1024, centuries before Europe's experimentation. An imperial government edict made paper money acceptable across the continent. This nurtured rising domestic trade through convenient notes redeemable against bronze and silver coins on demand.

The monetary regime aided regional unification and boosted the longevity of the Chinese empire. However, the influx of colonial British trade interference took hold by the late 1700s, sidelining native monetary system stability (Von Glahn, 2016). Banking credit and official tender notes were advanced financial intermediation instruments that facilitated trade mechanisms during the late Middle Ages. This led to the dramatic expansion of formidable economic frontiers.

The metallic predecessors of the florin and ducat, centuries earlier, foreshadowed the exponential leaps in money's innovative versatility. This enabled exploration, colonialism, early proto-globalization (Neal, 1990), and the transition away from closed-manor futures reliant on barter. Sophisticated credit and paper mechanisms became the primary catalysts for enriching open commerce possibilities. These mechanisms went beyond the severe limits of closed subsistence fiefdoms that were built solely upon awkward face-to-face commodity exchanges.

The triumph of merchant bankers over stubborn feudal lords became inexorable. This happened after the immensity of New

World bullion flows shifted power dynamics by enriching opportunist classes at the edge of the prevailing economic philosophy centered on stability through land and barter. People's ideas about the economy changed even more, and they started to support taking big risks in order to grow. This was possible with creative ways of setting up the money system that ancient times could never beat.

Money in the Modern Era

As transoceanic navigation flourished between the 15th and 18th centuries, international trade boomed enormously (Quinn, 2001). European colonial expeditions opened opportunities for wealthy merchant and financier interests to compete vigorously worldwide in plantations, slave trading, spices, textiles, etc.

Stockpiling scarce gold and silver became an overriding prerogative between rival empires, necessary for anchoring an expansive money supply to match their global ambitions. Thereby, they could bankroll expeditions through credible coinage and backing credit notes issued. These reserves crucially facilitated brisk trade growth as commerce networks transformed drastically in scale and dynamics (Neal, 1990).

When the Bank of England released paper banknotes in 1694, they took a big step forward in the portability of money. These notes could be exchanged for the amount of valuable metal stored in safe vaults (Flandreau, 2008). It was much easier to use this centralized indirect custody method than to physically move chunks of metal around for each transaction closure.

People could carry notes representing the gold's stored value instead. Paper banknotes accelerated commercial activity dramatically across England's immense maritime trade dominance. This dominance spanned worldwide colonies rich in resources, from the Americas to Asia. Overreach risks remained a constant threat due to the unbridled printing of notes.

Frequent financial panics and bank runs shattered depositor trust when promised metals proved insufficient against all outstanding papers. There were no longer any tangible assets to fully back this printing.

By the early 20th century, the classical Gold Standard had emerged as a widespread monetary regime.

Most major world economies rigidly tie their money supplies and price levels to their underlying quantities of national gold reserves (Eichengreen & Flandreau, 1997). Local paper currencies and bank credit notes were guaranteed convertibility into fixed amounts of gold, removing uncertainty between paper and tangible metal. Thereby, durable confidence rewarded the Gold Standard's financial discipline against wanton government overspending and currency manipulation. Using the golden factors, the exchange rates between countries' currencies were kept relatively stable. These currencies' values fluctuated based on each country's gold holdings, not short-term economic growth or political moves.

During the interwar period before WWII, European powers faced pressure to peg their currencies to the intrinsically strong US dollar instead of gold convertibility. Geostrategic interests also played an overriding factor in this situation (Lindert, 1969). After World War I, the US had the majority of world gold reserves, giving it unrivaled financial power and the ability to dictate conditions for exhausted allies.

Britain, in particular, faced no choice but to realign its currency's reliability with that of its Atlantic creditor nation. Gold remained the supreme monetary reserve asset internationally. However, pegging mechanisms evolved politically between governments due to the asymmetric distribution of actual bullion and bargaining dynamics, rather than purely currency market fluctuations.

Modern money has gone through three stages: coins from the colonial era, the peak of the Gold Standard, and the adjustment with dollar pegging. This pattern depicts how hard metallic tangibility, portable note convenience, and Machiavellian national ambitions battling for monetary authority using currencies as chess pieces interact. The never-ending dynamism between state financial leverage goals and everyday commercial stability requirements left citizens and institutions whipsawing amidst these macro-level feuds.

The Future of Money

Unrestricted fiat money production without commodity convertibility limits has increased money supply and debt in the post-gold standard era, according to Lee & Chan (2023). The lack of discipline is evident in the emperor's invisible clothes. Rampant inflation erodes the purchasing power and savings of ordinary citizens. It also benefits entrenched establishments through inflated asset prices and cheaper money paybacks.

Momentum has gradually gained from the evident failures of manipulated fiat regimes. This momentum aims to reintroduce reliable tangible assets with scarcity value, which could restore constraints against bad faith political debasements of currency value (Wu, 2017). Trust in authorities and institutions, historically relied upon as custodians of stability, has significantly deteriorated. This decline is due to their repeated flaunting of susceptibility for conflicts of interest and moral hazard at the expense of the public during recurring crises.

The innovation of Bitcoin represents a pivotal development harnessing digitization to address the apparent Achilles heels in previous monetary regimes, both fiat and commodities-backed. Bitcoin was launched anonymously in 2008, based on a significant whitepaper by Nakamoto. Peer-to-peer transaction validation and cryptographic protection make it work as a digital currency system. Additionally, it has a cap that an algorithm sets and that no one can change. This record of coin distribution is also available for public inspection.

This set of attributes offers the possibility for global direct value transfer without centralized intermediaries, upheld by intrinsic mathematical assurances rather than counterparty credibility.

Peer-to-peer transaction validation and cryptographic protection make it work as a digital currency system. Additionally, it has a cap that an algorithm sets and that no one can change. This record of coin distribution is also available for public inspection. However, whether Bitcoin escapes the same systemic corruption fate as oligarchic forces over time remains conjectural.

It has popularized the concept of advanced cryptography upholding financial honesty without relying on trusted human institutions. The use of antifragile programming in place of human discretion allows this to happen (Antonopoulos, 2017). At first, this information may shake people's beliefs about the need for "parents" to keep an eye on their finances.

When it comes to keeping money safe, central banks and private banks have their work cut out for them. However, Bitcoin and other decentralized cryptocurrency protocols could shake things up in the future (Buterin, 2020). These "trustless" standards show how to stop insiders from getting rich and the public from being put in danger over and over again, which is something that human institutions haven't been able to do. The rules are mathematically clear and don't depend on privilege.

According to monetary historians (Brands, 2022), this phenomenon's transparent decentralization does appear to be preparing the cyclic pendulum of regimes for structural transformation. Such protocols structurally discourage the re-emergence of parasitic rent-seeking intermediaries by removing gatekeepers offering little underlying value yet always attempting to tax creators. The creed matches nicely with parallel social shifts questioning old hierarchies.

Bitcoin and its underlying blockchain invention are still in the early stages, but they seem destined to play a role in the future of money. This poses dilemmas that legacy custodians can no longer dismiss. Digital gold is a complementary and safe haven asset, empowering internet-native micropayments and inspiring central bank digital currencies. Its principles grow internationally through digitalization alone, without the support of institutions.

Further miles remain on the marathon, but math and decentralization together appear poised to bolster financial accountability.

Bitcoin Potential as a Long-term Investment

As explored in the previous section, money fulfills the crucial functions of acting as a store of value and medium of exchange within economies. Money should maintain stable purchasing power over long horizons while enabling seamless transfers of value between parties. The monetary properties and evolutionary history of existing forms of money have been analysed over centuries. When judged against these criteria, the compelling investment case for Bitcoin becomes clear.

Bitcoin has become the leading monetary technology pioneer in just over a decade by reinventing internet-era money. A decentralized blockchain infrastructure and cryptography power the public transaction ledger known as bitcoin. Bitcoin is endowed with durability, security, and transparency. It enforces verifiable scarcity through an algorithmic schedule, capping the total units at 21 million.

In this section, we analyse the dimensions of Bitcoin's investment value proposition. We explore its monetary properties as emergent digital gold and its network effects that expand its usefulness and integration into mainstream finance.

What Makes a Successful Store of Value?

Effective stores of value reliably maintain purchasing power into the foreseeable future thanks to steady demand offsetting inflationary pressures. Key facets demanded from candidates considered for storing monetary value long-term include:

- **Durability:** persists decade after decade intact without substantial degradation
- **Portability/Conveyability:** Allows owners to securely transport wealth, including across borders
- **Fungibility:** Universal interchangeability between asset units to enable direct valuation
- **Verifiability:** Confirms authenticity rapidly to facilitate exchange between recipients
- **Scarcity:** Strictly capped supply conferring increasing value to fixed quantity
- **Censorship Resistance:** Shields use and possession rights against coercive third parties

Impervious Durability

Durable composition is paramount for any long-term store of value. It should be able to withstand the test of time, whether physically or digitally, without significant degradation. This will prevent permanent loss.

Consumptive assets like food commodities fail this test and cannot preserve intergenerational wealth. An effective multi-decade store of value must withstand years without eroding integrity, whether kept securely offline or actively used in trade and transactions.

Unbound Portability/Conveyability

Portability is crucial for any dominant monetary asset over decades and generations. It ensures seamless conveyance and inheritance transfer by securely transporting stores of value without logistical friction. Constraints around physical settlement risks or geographic controls over transferring value grow into liabilities failing this criterion. Scalable stores of value must move swiftly across locations or eras to successors without complex ownership exchanges through gatekeeping intermediaries.

Universal Fungibility Between Asset Units

Direct valuation and exchange necessitate fungibility, whereby specimens and measurable units demonstrate reliable interchangeability both upon scrutiny and during transactions. When individual units vary beyond reasonable tolerances or prove impossible to price precisely against market rates, overall tradability suffers across entire supply pools. Reluctancy emerges, treating unequal items equally. Thus, fungibility and the avoidance of discrimination among circulating supplies directly bolster liquidity depth, which is crucial for mature stores of value.

Rapid, Reliable Verification

Instant and reliable authentication is crucial for any store of value. It helps build confidence and ensures smooth transactions between recipients, minimising doubt or delays that can hinder trades. Lengthy, technically burdensome, or invasive verification approaches undermine asset acceptance and risk discouraging trade at the margins. Easy distinction between genuine and counterfeit specimens through accessible tools prevents dilution, compromising scarcity.

Censorship Resistance Upholding Peaceful Usage

Societal shifts towards financial surveillance infrastructures and restrictions over extending governmental control into civil economic activities highlight the rising importance of censorship resistance. Stores of value with properties preventing seizure or arbitrary interference by malicious external parties offer sanctuary for innocent owners. They protect possession rights and trade from coercive attacks and trade blocks that infringe upon essential liberties.

Bitcoin as Sound Money

Gold's physical chemistry limits inflation manipulability by central banks whimsically tinkering with interest rates, hoping to optimize dynamic, decentralized market economies centrally. Its physical nature restricts convertibility and necessitates expensive vaulting. Additionally, it faces constant debasement risks from fakes or financial instruments, creating excess paper claims on limited gold bars held in custody.

In resolute comparison, Bitcoin's trustless, instantly transmittable digital money breaches barbarous relic burdens while upholding everything that made gold sound like money for millennia. Bitcoin distills the best of gold's reliability and accessibility while vaulting magnitudes higher in performance metrics through clever cryptographic assurance. The coin essentially emerges as digital gold reinvented for the internet era. It possesses mathematically verifiable scarcity, decentralised production, a transparent public ledger, and censorship resistance, upholding permissionless transactional autonomy.

Bitcoin commands sound attributes that make it a credible storage refuge for wealth. Infinitely printable fiat central bank currencies such as dollars, euros, or yen are vulnerable to unrestrained inflationary politics. They undermine the core value function of money and become a liability due to predictable dilution.

Annual supply growth asymptotically trends to absolute 0% by 2140 when final coins from the maximum 21 million cap unlock. This ultra-hard supply schedule becomes economically embedded into the network's incentive structure and thus cannot be subverted without rendering Bitcoin valueless.

Bitcoin's borderless accessibility opens reliable wealth preservation to billions worldwide through uncensorable transactions. Additionally, unlike traditional assets siloed within singular legal jurisdictions or banking geographies, encrypting and shattering keys across devices or memorizing seed passphrases, even confiscation against totalitarian regimes fails to force access. This novel self-custodial model retires the risks historically intrinsic to entrusting money security to centralized third-party vaults.

Investment Use Case and Network Effects

Beyond sound money properties attracting conviction buys from long-term investors, Bitcoin's rapidly expanding transactional utility and various indirect network effects fuel a self-reinforcing virtuous adoption cycle, making its global multi-trillion-dollar market value milestone seem just the beginning.

Direct use cases powering Bitcoin investment go beyond speculative trading on dollar-denominated exchanges. Many people around the world experience unreliable domestic currencies and frequent wealth confiscation, along with capital controls. Accessible, borderless money provides financial freedom from corrupt regimes. Citizens from Venezuela to Lebanon switched savings into "digital gold," hoping wealth would retain future purchasing power despite the national currency collapse.

Bitcoin's blockchain transparency allows for faster and cheaper settlement finality in commercial trade. This is in contrast to conventional institutional arrangements that are hindered by the political risks associated with nation-state-regulated transaction channels.

Global merchants and supply chain operators are increasingly denominating deals in Bitcoin. This eliminates the need for correspondent banking relationships or currency conversions through sanctioned dollar hegemony guardrails. Open-source money thus effectively disintermediates legacy finance, even for mainstream commercial operators.

Bitcoin's expanding role as a decentralised global trade settlement network is growing alongside its developing world adoption. Underbanked populations fighting against unreliable sovereign currencies as a result of poorly managed monetary policies are the driving force behind this adoption. Its open blockchain architecture offers an alternative to conventional finance plagued by political risks, currency controls, and dependencies on nation-state-regulated transaction channels.

Bitcoin enables direct merchant value transfer without the need for centralised gatekeepers or toll takers, eliminating fees associated with correspondent banking relationships. This immunity from systemic dependencies reduces costs for global trade and remittances.

Its transparent ledger enables reliable jurisdictional finality for commercial payments, while programmability supports automation and optimizes logistic workflows. Companies leveraging these benefits incrementally uncouple from degrading fiat monopolies and strengthen the circular network effects benefiting Bitcoin's investment viability.

Innovative corporate treasurers are now gradually and irreversibly re-denominating deals directly in borderless digital currency. This eliminates the need for conversions through sanctioned money like US dollars, which historically dominated international trade due to its privileged hegemony. But open monetary networks naturally erode such inefficiencies as software optimizes around optionality, transparency, and direct reconciliation across all counterparties.

Distressed populations worldwide are switching domestic savings into perceived haven assets like Bitcoin. This is done to escape political troubles debasing national currencies, which also expands network effects. New categories of users adopt Bitcoin's investment use cases, motivated by self-preservation rather than speculative trading. This boosts liquidity depth, incentivizes financial product development, and ultimately matures this novel asset class towards establishment legitimacy over its current speculative adolescence.

The History of Bitcoin Price

Bitcoin is not just a digital currency; it's a phenomenon that has reshaped the financial landscape since its inception. The history of Bitcoin is pivotal for understanding its current value and potential future. It was conceived as a decentralized alternative to traditional currencies, a digital form of money that uses cryptography to control its creation and management rather than relying on central authorities.

Bitcoin price history: from $0 to $1

In Bitcoin's earliest era, the nascent cryptographic creation lacked a formalized pricing mechanism. On October 5th, 2009, the New Liberty Standard helped catalyze wider adoption by publishing the first public Bitcoin exchange rate, valuing the decentralized digital currency at $0.000764 per unit. This dollar conversion meant an astonishing 1,309 BTC could be purchased for just $1 at the time. Though rudimentary, this initial rate kickstarted Bitcoin's slow emergence from the shadows of cypherpunk forums towards more mainstream recognition and trading activity.

During its first developmental phase from 2009 to 2011, Bitcoin's early journey centered around cultivation by a small but passionate niche constituency of cryptography experts, libertarians, technology pioneers, and digital activists who were drawn to the experimental cryptocurrency's promise of decentralized governance and permissionless peer-to-peer transactions without centralized intermediaries.

Kickstarting real-world Bitcoin integration, one of the most publicized events occurred in 2010 when early adopter Laszlo Hanyecz conducted the first physical transaction, exchanging 10,000 bitcoins for two Papa John's pizzas. While deemed trivial at the time, valued at only around $30, this became an iconic moment and, over the years, came to symbolize Bitcoin's extraordinary upside potential, with those 10,000 coins worth millions today.

Other integral milestones rapidly succeeded one another, compounding technological strides as Bitcoin permeated further into the public consciousness after catching the curiosity of major media outlets and tech behemoths. Shielding the protocol, Version 0.3 of the reference Bitcoin client software launched in mid-2010, harboring critical security enhancements. Meanwhile, by early 2011, the pioneering Bitcoin Market exchange had activated, now succeeded by the Mt.Gox exchange, which shortly began facilitating over 70% of all Bitcoin transactions by the year's end, cementing critical infrastructure and supporting growth.

Laying the groundwork for Bitcoin's future disruptive impact, this formative 2009-2011 period planted pivotal building blocks through breakthroughs on multiple fronts, both technically and commercially, while nascent investment and trading activity started blossoming within enthusiast circles.

Bitcoin price history: from $1 to $200 (2010-2013)

A significant milestone emerged in June 2011 when Bitcoin's price spiked to around $30, reaching this psychological barrier for the first time before plunging sharply back down. There was a period of relative stabilization rather than collapse after this brief peak. It formed an orderly base period, helping establish Bitcoin's resiliency while setting the stage for further upside. Investor interest continued to gather momentum, foreshadowing additional growth.

The timeframe between 2011 and 2013 proved pivotal in Bitcoin's coming of age. By achieving parity with the US dollar in February 2011, Bitcoin's perception evolved from being a solely experimental digital currency to cementing credibility as a burgeoning new-age asset class attracting investor dollars. Consequently, media outlets stepped up coverage of Bitcoin's foray into mainstream finance. As public awareness expanded exponentially, interest and demand followed suit. Accelerating price gains ultimately culminated in a vertical price spike topping out above $200 by April 2013. However, early euphoria soon confronted reality.

During its formative years, Bitcoin also endured setbacks typical of untested markets. Volatility ran high alongside uncertainty. For example, following the aforementioned price peak in June 2011 above $30, Bitcoin plunged abruptly after a high-profile security incident at the Mt. Gox exchange temporarily eroded fragile investor confidence. This early crypto trading pioneer suffered a debilitating hack, catalyzing concerns about security and stability.

Nevertheless, Bitcoin's revolutionary underpinning technology and paradigm-shifting promise buoyed its prospects among early adopters, who were optimistic about its long-term disruption potential despite intermittent turbulence. Indentations like the Mt. Gox breach spawned setbacks but failed to derail growing enthusiasm among investors willing to stomach volatility in return for asymmetric upside. Progress marched forward.

Consequently, 2011-2013 saw increased integration of Bitcoin into the fabric of digital financial transactions via the establishment of associated businesses catering to cryptocurrency needs. These promising developments extended Bitcoin's accessibility further for speculators and enthusiasts drawn to crypto ideology and libertarian values.

Later, the 2012-2013 Cyprus banking crisis amplified Bitcoin's appeal globally by underscoring the vulnerabilities inherent in centralized traditional banking. As depositors endured frozen accounts and enforced capital controls, demand for censorship-resistant currency alternatives like Bitcoin intensified dramatically. Responding strongly to these dynamics, Bitcoin entered another vertiginous price ascent, blowing past its 2011 highs before topping out above $200 leading into 2013.

In summary, the transitional 2011-2013 phase cemented Bitcoin's validity through growing mainstream recognition and rapid value accretion. Once widely dismissed as a nerdy novelty, Bitcoin emerged from these formative years and was increasingly considered a serious asset class and revolutionary monetary system challenger that was here to stay, despite lingering skepticism.

Bitcoin price history: from $200 to $20,000 (2010-2018)

The evolution of Bitcoin's valuation from 2013 to 2017 proves extraordinary. Bitcoin's ascent, while volatile, mirrored the trajectory of disruptive technologies battling for acceptance in the mainstream.

In 2013, Bitcoin prices fluctuated dramatically. Prices rocketed upward in orbit due to rising interest, shocking skeptics by crossing the $1,000 mark by November. However, it was no smooth ride skyward. Powerful crosscurrents buffeted Bitcoin's ascent. Surging interest from China and escalating adoption for completing international transactions provided tailwinds towards the Bitcoin price's stratospheric rise. But countervailing regulatory headwinds, especially China's escalating hostile posture, led to whipsawing selloffs, battering prices, and spotlighting Bitcoin's sensitivity to government actions during its developmental phase.

The following year, in 2014, Bitcoin contended with even more ferocious regulatory headwinds and reputation-shattering industry turmoil. Most notoriously, the collapse of Mt. Gox, an early leading Bitcoin exchange, devastated confidence, while ongoing legal gray zones suppressed prices. This year marked a period of painful maturation rather than exuberance. While disheartening to investors, the Mt. Gox debacle did instill critical infrastructure improvements and security reinforcement initiatives across exchanges worldwide, promoting long-term ecosystem integrity at the expense of short-term returns. Outside of prices, critical technological advancements like multi-signature Bitcoin wallets also materialized, beginning to shift sentiment by underscoring Bitcoin's tangible utility advantages.

After a muted 2015 spent mostly consolidating and slowly recovering reputational damage inflicted during the prior year's chaos, Bitcoin's true breakthrough emerged in 2016, marking the watershed moment when Bitcoin's revolutionary ethos transitioned slowly towards mainstream legitimacy. This pivotal transformation came as political instability shocked establishment trust worldwide. Events like Brexit, along with the unprecedented devaluation of the Chinese yuan currency, spotlighted Bitcoin's appeal as a decentralized digital safe haven to protect capital from centralized institutional failings worldwide. Against the global backdrop of intensifying distrust in traditional pillars of stability, cypherpunk experiment no more, Bitcoin assumed the mantle of digital gold-a stateless, censorship-resistant store of value for the digital age. This psychological transition powered Bitcoin's value to fresh heights.

Thereafter, Bitcoin's trajectory in 2017 proved parabolic as a confluence of now well-documented tailwinds propelled Bitcoin firmly into the global asset class stratosphere. Widespread media hype, proliferating ICO mania, Wall Street and institutional investor flirtation, and exchange infrastructure scaling drew the world's fervent attention. Retail investors stampeded into Bitcoin as blockchain technology permeated global business and financial conversations, driving the expanding crypto industry and decentralization movement and luring them in with spectacular returns and its sudden legitimacy as an uncorrelated, high-octane asset class. By late December, this perfect storm culminated with Bitcoin reaching unprecedented peaks arobefore000 - before the winds shifted the other way.

Bitcoin history: 2010-2023

The aftermath of the crypto fever pitch in 2017 gave way to a punishing bear market throughout 2018, as Bitcoin values deteriorated substantially. Multiple factors catalyzed this reversal, including intensified regulatory scrutiny of crypto activities worldwide, a series of high-profile cyberattacks on various exchanges, and a tapering off from the state of frenzied speculation as investors grew cautious after getting burned. As the dust settled from the ripping bull run and subsequent comedown, the crypto markets stabilized, and Bitcoin in particular gradually regained its footing in 2019 with steadier, more sustainable growth. Momentum built as Bitcoin started showing signs of a renewed recovery.

The unprecedented economic crisis triggered by the COVID-19 pandemic in 2020 marked a pivotal juncture, as an atmosphere of uncertainty and currency devaluation helped shine a spotlight on Bitcoin as a potential safe haven asset. No longer confined to the fringes, Bitcoin stepped further into the mainstream as a digital analog to gold, attracting significant new investment inflows while acting as an inflation hedge. These macro conditions powered

Bitcoin prices to breakthrough to fresh all-time highs. At the same time, intensifying institutional interest gained traction, bolstering Bitcoin's credibility in the process.

2021 turned out to be a banner year for Bitcoin thanks to increased adoption and endorsements from influential corporate and financial figures. Major businesses ranging from PayPal to AT&T, as well as influential investors like Paul Tudor Jones, integrated crypto payment options and allocated Bitcoin as an inflation hedge. Furthermore, the advent of the first US Bitcoin ETFs lowered barriers for more traditional retail and institutional investors to gain exposure by removing direct custody challenges. Propelled higher by these catalysts, Bitcoin prices soared to the cusp of $70,000—just shy of hitting the psychologically important milestone before retreating.

In 2022, the bears took hold once again, with Bitcoin prices cratering over 60% from the prior year's peaks. As tightening monetary policy and concerns over a global economic slowdown rattled markets, Bitcoin plunged precipitously to around $16,000 by November. Prone to violent boom and bust cycles, Bitcoin traded rangebound between $16,000 and $30,000 for almost a year as investors braced for prolonged crypto winter conditions.

However, the tide started shifting in Q4 of 2023 as inflation concerns re-emerged, boosting Bitcoin's appeal anew as central bank policies came under fire. Investor sentiment pivoted positively, fueling renewed momentum that powered Bitcoin decisively back above the $40,000 resistance. As the year draws to a close, Bitcoin appears to be regaining its appreciation, trading around $38,000 to $44,000, though whether bullish momentum endures remains an open question given the ever-present volatility.

Key facts about the history of the Bitcoin price

The historical trajectory of Bitcoin's price is a testament to its volatility and the transformative impact it has had on the concept of money and investment. Here are some key facts that punctuate its history:

All-Time High

On November 10, 2021, Bitcoin reached its highest valuation ever, hitting $68,789.63 after a remarkable ascent. This long-awaited pinnacle event represented a historic milestone—an astronomical gain of over 1,000,000% from Bitcoin's inception over a decade prior at fractions of a penny. This fact underscores the exponential, albeit volatile, growth that has propelled Bitcoin from its roots as an obscure digital experiment to the influential asset class it has become. For proponents, this achievement validates Bitcoin's staying power, while for skeptics, it epitomizes a speculative mania detached from fundamentals. Regardless of perspective, this all-time high price punctuates Bitcoin's transformational impact on finance and investment.

Steepest Single-Day Decline

Bitcoin's susceptibility to sudden, severe price moves was starkly highlighted on May 19, 2022, when the price plunged 20.5% within a 24-hour period. This startling collapse saw Bitcoin fall from $36,950 to $29,737, lopping off billions in market value practically instantly. This one-day evaporation of over $7,000 demonstrates the gut-wrenching downside risk of Bitcoin's hyper-volatility. While volatility can multiply profits during good times, it can also violently reverse course—a reality that long-term crypto investors must psychologically and financially brace for. Crashes of this magnitude illustrate why Bitcoin day-trading remains largely the purview of sophisticated risk-tolerant traders rather than casual dabblers.

Largest Single-Day Price Increase

On November 10, 2021, the very same day Bitcoin reached its headline-grabbing all-time high, it also recorded its steepest ever single-day price ascent. Within 24 hours, Bitcoin's price catapulted a shocking 17.8%, jumping from $58,958 to $68,789. This rapid advance demonstrates Bitcoin's ability to generate tremendous paper gains in an astonishingly short timeframe. However, timing entries and exits amidst extreme intraday swings requires great skill and discipline. Bitcoin has always been a rollercoaster ride, capable of life-changing rallies for seasoned investors but also gut-wrenching corrections that can erase months of progress in hours for the overzealous.

These examples of extreme volatility encapsulate the double-edged sword of crypto investing. The prospect of rapid wealth creation dangles tantalizingly close at all times but is often yanked away unexpectedly, leaving many powerless to react in time. Ultimately, Bitcoin's price extremes serve as an ongoing reminder of the "high-risk, high-reward" crypto mantra that continues to ring true.

These key moments encapsulate the extreme highs and lows of Bitcoin's price history and serve as a stark illustration of the high-risk, high-reward nature of cryptocurrency investment.

The annual return on Bitcoin investments

From 2013 through 2023, Bitcoin has posted an astonishing average annual return of 230%. This remarkable performance far surpasses many traditional investment vehicles over the past decade. To put this extraordinary growth into perspective, let's examine Bitcoin's actual annual returns year-by-year and compare them to stocks and gold:

In the challenging year of 2022, Bitcoin investors faced steep losses, with a negative return of -58.1%. This severe drop reflected the broad turbulence in financial markets and deteriorating macroeconomic conditions that accelerated the crypto bear market.

By contrast, 2021 was a standout year for Bitcoin, with healthy gains of 64.8%. This robust return was fueled by rapidly increasing institutional adoption, as major corporations and financial players entered the crypto space. Mainstream interest exploded, providing tailwinds.

The unprecedented economic events triggered by the global pandemic in 2020 led to a flood of investment into Bitcoin, yielding outsized returns of 300%. As uncertainty rocked markets, investors sought out digital safe havens, perceiving Bitcoin as a hedge against the broader macro turmoil.

In 2019, Bitcoin's return moderated but remained strong at 91.7%, as it steadily recovered ground after the preceding year's plunge. Investor confidence improved progressively through the year.

2018 marked a difficult period for Bitcoin investors, as prices corrected sharply, culminating in an annual loss of -75.2%. This followed the euphoric boom and bust of 2017's historic crypto bubble.

2017 was arguably the banner year for Bitcoin returns, posting a staggering gain of 2,221.8%, despite the correction at year-end. As public awareness exploded, frenzied speculative mania fuelled this upside.

Building on growing confidence in its potential, Bitcoin gained 130.9% in 2016. This marked an inflection point for more mainstream recognition.

In 2015, Bitcoin returns were steadier, coming in at 47.1% annually, as adoption increased measurably, though mainstream traction remained elusive.

By comparison, mainstream investments like stocks and gold have delivered far more modest returns over the long term. For instance, when adjusting for inflation, the stock market has historically yielded average annualized returns of around 7–10%.

Meanwhile, gold, long considered the archetypal stable asset, typically increases in value at approximately the rate of inflation over time. This has resulted in markedly lower returns than Bitcoin, albeit with far less volatility.

These comparisons serve to highlight Bitcoin's astronomical upside in certain years, dwarfing most traditional assets. However, they also underscore its penchant for extreme volatility, vulnerability to investor sentiment, and sensitivity to evolving regulatory regimes.

What factors influence the bitcoin price history?

The interplay of various factors affects Bitcoin's price history, with speculation, adoption, and regulation standing out as the most significant. Each of these factors can have both short-term and long-term effects on Bitcoin's price, contributing to its volatility and unique market dynamics. Understanding the interplay between speculation, adoption, and regulation is crucial for anyone looking to interpret Bitcoin's price movements and the cryptocurrency market as a whole.

Speculation Impact on Bitcoin Prices

As a nascent asset class lacking clear valuation models, Bitcoin prices have proven highly receptive to speculative market influence from traders and investors. Driven by emotions like fear and greed rather than grounded in fundamental analysis, speculative trading decisions tend to rely on sentiment and expectations of future price movements. During periods of euphoria, this can ignite powerful bull runs and parabolic rallies like that seen in 2017 before the massive bubble popped. Conversely, panicked selling can induce precipitous price declines when optimism turns to pessimism. By nature, decentralized and borderless, Bitcoin speculation occurs 24/7 across global exchanges, amplifying volatility.

Adoption Effects on Bitcoin Valuation

While speculators squabble over anticipated price moves, Bitcoin's valuation has also historically climbed alongside increased adoption rates as its overall circulation grows more useful in daily life. The more individuals, businesses, and organizations accept and acquire Bitcoin for payments, investments, or other purposes, the more its acquisition demand rises against limited new supply, applying upward pressure on prices. Mainstream corporate and institutional adoption represent key milestones, lending Bitcoin credibility and stability, which typically unlocks a surge of new entrants fearful of missing out. Events leading to direct access for Wall Street investors, like the approval of the first US Bitcoin futures and Bitcoin ETFs, similarly stoked bull markets as barriers to entry were lowered. If Bitcoin adoption reverts or stalls, downside risk exists.

Regulatory Impact on Bitcoin Market Dynamics

As the regulatory fate of Bitcoin remains fluid across different countries, announcements or hints of new policies from governments and financial regulators produce outsize influence over Bitcoin's price swings by altering perceptions of future feasibility and legality. Historically, crackdowns from China or restrictive policies from India have dealt blows to Bitcoin prices by seeding doubts, whereas embracing gestures from Switzerland or El Salvador electrified the market by inspiring followers. While decentralized in nature, Bitcoin exchanges and related service providers constitute vulnerabilities susceptible to localized enforcement actions, as demonstrated after South Korean restrictions caused broad-based selling. Since Bitcoin transcends borders, it generally resurrects eventually but regulatory spotlights spook easily panicked investors awaiting greater clarity around acceptable uses.

Pros of bitcoin pricing

Decentralization and Promoting Organic Price Discovery: A major structural advantage underpinning Bitcoin's pricing model is its decentralized architecture, free from centralized control. Unlike fiat currencies like the US dollar, which central banks can candidate at will without limit, Bitcoin's issuance adheres to algorithmic protocol rules transparent for all to analyze. This insulation from artificial manipulation engenders organic price discovery dynamics akin to commodities like gold where prices respond directly to demand fluctuations rather than arbitrary decisions by bureaucrats. In times of financial instability triggered by irresponsible policies endangering national currencies, Bitcoin has historically provided a life raft for investors seeking shelter in deflationary assets disconnected from the incumbent failing system.

Scarcity-Driven Value Accrual Over Time: Additionally, Bitcoin's intrinsically scarce supply controlled by protocols with only 21 million units ever issued appeals to investors with a low time preference valuing hard money qualities. The transparently fixed cap invokes the stock-to-flow models often applied to precious metals where predictably decreasing production increases scarcity hence value over time. With lost Bitcoin inaccessible forever and each halving event decreasing daily minted supply by half, Bitcoin's network value may continue appreciating indefinitely as long as demand increases to absorb the declining daily inflows. This remains an enticing value proposition for holders with long investment horizons.

Cons of bitcoin pricing

Volatility Vulnerabilities from Sentiment Shifts: Unfortunately, disadvantages exist too that introduce pricing fragilities. Bitcoin's fully decentralized nature means no stabilizing central entity can intervene to dampen excessive volatility driven by irrational exuberance or capitulation cascades. Speculation-fueled bubbles are also a byproduct since Bitcoin lacks fundamentals to anchor prices during times of mass hysteria. Furthermore, extreme correlations with highly speculative tech stocks plagued Bitcoin as tightly coupled assets sell off indiscriminately during turbulent market episodes. Until Bitcoin's liquidity matures and its investor base broadens, temporary dislocations and extended bear markets may continue testing patience.

Exogenous Risks Like Unexpected Policy Shifts: Importantly, as Bitcoin investors realized after abrupt Chinese mining bans shocked markets, exogenous regulatory pronouncements can overwhelm organic price drivers, introducing destabilizing risks difficult to model or predict. As decentralized technology collides with territorial policymakers and entrenched financial incumbents wielding guns and badges, political whims sway Bitcoin's price trajectory, especially locally within jurisdictions like India. However, Bitcoin's antifragility shines over lengthy timeframes as crackdowns typically catalyze relocation without undermining network integrity. Still, risks remain ever-present. So do price whipsaws.

Summary

In its first 14 years since inception, the price of Bitcoin has climbed over one million times from its initial negligible value to reaching an apex of nearly $69,000 per coin in late 2021. This extraordinary ascent reflects the profound, if often misunderstood, allure of Bitcoin as a scarce digital asset with embedded properties seemingly tailor-made to serve as "digital gold" and a revolutionary challenger to traditional financial rails. However, monumental growth has not come without substantial growing pains and challenges that continue plaguing the Bitcoin ecosystem. Specifically, Bitcoin's price history has been notoriously volatile, with the potential for dizzying price spikes but also massive, rapid sell-offs within short timeframes. This radical volatility remains Bitcoin's double-edged sword - offering opportunities for tremendous wealth creation but also posing substantial risk for investors unable to stomach freefalls exceeding 50 percent crashes in value. As Bitcoin continues the complex process of maturation and integration into the broader global financial landscape, it remains a beacon of both the astonishing potential but also inherent pitfalls in these still nascent cryptocurrency markets.

Path Towards Mainstream Adoption as Medium of Exchange

Critics argue that Bitcoin's volatility makes it challenging to use as a daily spendable currency for pricing goods and services. Counterarguments suggest that Bitcoin's ultimate destiny is more as digital gold, accumulating inheritable wealth over generations. It is not primarily intended for coffee purchases, where convenience takes precedence over the need for inflation hedging.

Bitcoin's blockchain facilitates programmable money innovations. It addresses earlier technology and user experience limitations, regardless of debates about whether it qualifies by today's currency thresholds.

Secured lending against bitcoin holdings enables spending power without requiring the sale of saved assets. Exchanges and wallets now issue fiat-pegged stablecoins, like tether, roundtripping the desired medium of exchange stability by collateralizing original volatile coins still owned. Identity-verified debit cards allow leveraging small percentages of cryptocurrency wealth on wallet apps to tap spending needs similar to credit cards.

Scalability is achieved by processing millions of low-value transactions in batches on the Lightning Network's rail channels. These transactions have minimal fees at settlement and still maintain the secure nature of Bitcoin's blockchain.

The graduating ecosystem of solutions built surrounding Bitcoin echoes how TCP/IP bootstrapped the internet. It required complementary browsers, encryption, responsiveness, accessibility, and e-commerce tools to realise ubiquitous usage over successive buildout decades. Today's frustrations ignore computing's immaturity in Bitcoin's decade-first phase supporting this base layer rail network tracking value. The next decade promises to crush barriers towards institutions, enterprises, and consumers interfacing with the crypto economy. This will be as easy as using incumbent services.

Essentially, arguments insisting money always necessitates centralized issuer backing ignore blockchain's transformation, securing trustless direct exchange online. Bitcoin's decentralised global transfer network fulfils promises of attracting internet proliferation, boosting human connectivity, and democratising information. It is freed from institutional burdens and barriers, revolutionising money and finance.

Bitcoin maintains its core principle of decentralisation. It also makes progress in gaining widespread recognition and integration with existing financial services through the use of various emerging access and technology solutions. Developments like Lightning Network may eventually moot earlier concerns around volatility or transactional capacity faced by natively digital, decentralized money in its infancy.

Economic incentives have a greater influence than policy on the long-term patterns of technological disruption and adoption. Temporary debates in political or public circles, which may lack understanding of the intricacies of financial innovation, do not alter this fact.

The open blockchain architecture allowed Bitcoin to maintain its decentralised nature during 13 years of stress testing and adversarial environments. The surrounding ecosystem of Bitcoin thrives on modular innovation rather than monolithic decree. Progressive solutions tackling adoption obstacles at consumer and institutional levels organically emerge through market fitness and incentives. The cumulative momentum promises that this following decade will likely crush most barriers toward wider maturity.

Comparing Bitcoin to Traditional Assets

Bitcoin's viability within the emerging cryptocurrency asset category can be analysed. A comparative lens can be used to contrast its attributes against traditional investment staples like stocks, gold, and real estate. This can illuminate outlier properties and signal huge yet underexplored potential being mispriced by status quo financial paradigms.

Bitcoin's distinctive edge becomes pronounced across various evaluation metrics, including risk and return profiles, structural composition, and conveyability advantages. Its portfolio utility demonstrates uncanny resilience even amidst shakes rippling traditional markets. A decade ago, an unfamiliar digital asset vehicle was sceptically received at the fringe. Now, it commands growing legitimacy and challenges assumptions that uphold legacy assets taken for granted.

Bitcoin vs Stocks

Stocks represent fractional ownership claims to a company that are expected to generate economic profits. Bitcoin establishes direct title rights on a scarce public ledger. It symbolises monetary value secured by cryptography and computing force, effectively creating digital gold.

Bitcoin's antifragile Lindy network effects cement further over each wave of reflexive valuation. The network is also attracted to its game theoretically locked-in proposition, unlike enterprises perpetually competing against disruption.

Equities factor productive human ingenuity endlessly iterating on goods and services, answering unsatisfied needs before competitors. Bitcoin specifically constructs a parallel recalibration of money. This recalibration becomes necessitated by unsustainable social harms induced by unfettered fiat debasement, livestock herding citizenry towards overconsumption even against conscience.

Stocks swell from capital flows seeking temporary parking in corporate vehicles economically isolated except financial reporting. Bitcoin also swells, attracting demonetized inhabitants into lifeboats whose viability and occupancy rate mutually scale on community resilience demonstrated across thirteen years undefeated against unrelenting opposition, scepticism, and slander.

Equity investing requires trust in opaque corporate governance and intermediary risks, such as insider self-dealing, third-party documentation fraud, or clearing firm continuity assumptions. Bitcoin enables direct peer-to-peer exchange without permissions, seizure, censorship, or terms of service adjustments. This ensures full sovereign possession rights and showcases Antifragile credibility that corporations cannot attain due to human discretion, managerial hierarchies, or shareholder voting facades.

This contrarian entrant has recorded almost parabolic 1900% annualised gains since inception. However, key metrics assessing risk and return dynamics reveal vast performance divergences favouring it over wider stock investing.

Bitcoin's volatility arises from the two-sided auction that determines its fair value as an unprecedented asset class. The mentioned volatility differs from the volatility in business operations. This contradicts the desires of patient shareholders who seek sustainable compound growth through long-term consumer loyalty.

Incorporating a small 1-6% bitcoin allocation in a stock portfolio significantly enhances risk-adjusted returns. This is due to the low correlations with other asset categories, which protect the overall portfolio from drawdowns, as mentioned by Aaron Brown's "constructive ambiguity."

The S&P 500 is close to reaching its all-time-high plateaus, while Bitcoin is still 70% below its highest valuation. This creates a starkly asymmetrical risk/reward profile, with Bitcoin gaining legitimacy from the establishment after being denied for over a decade.

Gold was conveniently banned in 1934, but later regained its global money status as Guardians. The rise of digital entrants, which cannot be effectively censored or contained by legislation, led to the decline of Towering.

Open water exists in the Pacific Ocean of cryptocurrency, possibly rising an order higher before even matching combined precious metals market capitalization. The Bitcoin black hole makes almost no industry future-proof. It directly homogenises a higher share of global liquidity pools into base settlement layer protocols. It does not rely on old world aggregators such as commercial banking or asset management rent seekers.

Bitcoin vs Gold

Gold and Bitcoin are both forms of monetary energy that are deliberately protected from unrestricted inflationary manipulation. They are distinct from infinitely dilutable paper currency, which constantly loses value when compared to enduring frames of reference.

Bitcoin mathematically caps circulation and introduces trustless direct custody, challenging state coercion. It carries gold's sound money banner into the instant digital realm, remaining resilient against forced seizure, transaction censorship, or clandestine wealth erosion via negative rate policies. It provides a refuge beyond establishment control for the global citizenry.

While gold fulfills desirable properties like indestructibility and supreme scarcity, it severely trails conveyability, security, auditability, and settlement finality in a modern context. Vault storage requires trusting fragile human guardians. Slow and insecure physical transportation channels expose themselves to risks of loss from interdiction, disasters, or documentation failures, particularly across borders.

Destructive abrasive testing methods are required for gold verifiability. Bitcoin's transparent signature-based blockchain allows tracing a valid chain of custody back to the genesis block. However, it leaves syntax wriggle room.

Gold faces physical restraints, while Bitcoin enables instant peer-to-peer transactions using self-custody cryptography. This ensures identical authenticity. There is no need for trusted intermediaries. Historically, intermediaries have been associated with moral hazards and rent extraction. This is due to conflicted custody incentives and fractional reserves that encourage mismatches against outstanding claims.

Bitcoin's fixed terminal supply allows for peer-level direct asset ownership to be checked cryptographically. This resists the constraints imposed by centralised authority, which has historically been a common breeding ground for insatiable wealth extraction ambitions.

Gold has limited industrial use cases, while Bitcoin enables a parallel economy with programmable money utilities that enhance functionality, versatility, and convenience. This attracts growing network effects beyond being just a store of value. Decentralized cryptocurrency exchanges destabilise geographic arbitrage schemes. These schemes previously forced global trade through monopolist toll takers, who charged privileges for capital flight agencies or access to banking conveniences.

Crypto whale wallets, which are denominated in Bitcoin instead of national currency, provide better high-net-worth insurance and inheritance planning. This is in contrast to allocated bullion or diamond heirlooms, which are susceptible to seizure or conflicted intermediation.

Bitcoin's accessible user experiences and meme-friendly adoption incentives resonate strongly with younger, digitally native populations. These populations are already comfortable with internet platform abstractions and appreciate Bitcoin's underlying decentralisation ethos. This test of time overpowers gold.

The trillion-dollar insurance value remains an elusive milestone for this monetary moonshot asset. However, there are no laws of physics that limit its eventual ascent if expanding bullish narratives fulfil cycling feedback loops enrolling incoming wealth inflows.

CHAPTER 3:

The Future of Bitcoin and Crypto in General

Bitcoin's revolutionary potential has become evident, though mainstream traction has remained elusive. This chapter analyzes the imminent catalysts priming cryptocurrency for widespread adoption alongside proliferating use cases destabilizing traditional finance. Intermediary gatekeeping enforced arbitrary constraints against peer economic agency for too long. Now, mathematically inclusive architectures herald emancipation.

Centralized toll-takers across banking, social media, and content creation monopolized captive audiences through credentialism. Insurgent permissionless protocols now directly connect willing counterparties using elegant cryptography for digital trust minimization instead of coercion. Bitcoin sparked this digital reformation as sound internet-native money, ensuring incorruptible value conveyance ethically secured by consensus incentives.

Upcoming cyclical code milestones guaranteeing increasing supply scarcity should drive mainstream interest, particularly if met alongside regulatory clarity. Exponentially expanding token functionality unlocks self-sovereign decentralized services. This transition of economic gravity into user-centric Web 3.0 paradigms fulfills the decentralized global financial network envisaged upon Bitcoin's 2008 origination.

Promise materialized slowly through the crypto winter spanning 2018–2020 amidst dismissive skeptics. But in hindsight, the disciplining cooldown forged antifragility that is now being tested with aplomb. Inevitably, some speculative froth requires pruning during irrational exuberance peaks before enduring foundations solidify. Patience combined with conviction redounds positively, given sufficient time horizons, if steadfast principles hold constant.

Bitcoin and cryptocurrency have already come incredibly far in their first decade, providing digital economic freedom. Mainstream visibility remained limited like the earliest internet, confined within niche realms of hobbyists and academics before exponentially expanding through irresistible grassroots utility. This long-arc trajectory stays intact as user onboarding smooths through better interfaces, financial instruments, and jurisdictional regulation, welcoming permissionless innovation over reactive prohibition.

Mainstream Adoption of Bitcoin

Increasing Wall Street titans openly praise Bitcoin's role as digital gold, a novel asset class, and a promising alternative to depreciating currencies vulnerable to spendthrift regimes. These institutions allocate investment capital directly where markets expand next. Their shifting favor signals widening acceptance after dismissiveness just years prior from entrenched incumbents protecting status quo mindshare.

Pension funds and university endowments allocate minor Bitcoin assets to diversify against inflation and systemic risks uncorrelated with stock and bond allocations. Their endorsement grants implicit legitimacy that the underlying blockchain technology passed rigorous due diligence, proving long-term viability prospects.

El Salvador adopted Bitcoin as parallel legal tender in 2021. This decision aimed to streamline remittances and bypass intermediary friction, which often resulted in high transaction fees for citizens sending earnings home from overseas. The embrace hints at wider sovereign adoption by countries with high inflationary regimes and reliance upon remittances, where Bitcoin conveys advantages over existing channels.

Public corporations like Tesla and MicroStrategy allocated billions to purchase Bitcoin for corporate treasury reserve assets. This move aims to protect shareholder value from potential currency debasement. Their allocations to digital gold mirror similar transitions away from dollar dependence towards immutably scarce Bitcoin. These decisive moves pressure comparable organizations to follow lest they trail peers creatively insulating balance sheets early.

Mainstream media skeptically framed crypto as play money for internet nerds just years ago before intense 2021 FOMO spotlighted 1,000%+ returns over a decade's compounding. High risk accompanies high reward during the initial growth phases of pioneering any novel disruptive technology. But accumulating strengths establish a widening moat as network effects take hold through the classic S-curve lifecycle trajectory that internet protocols exhibited before crypto.

Expanding crypto financial products

Bitcoin exchange-traded funds (ETFs) offer institutional and retail investors exposure to Bitcoin without the complexities of directly holding cryptocurrency. However, United States regulators have historically rejected numerous Bitcoin ETF filings, cautious of potential manipulation harming investors.

The SEC maintains dual mandates governing financial innovation - consumer protection and market integrity. However, their prudent restraint often heavily favors status quo incumbents, hindering progress by erecting regulatory moats and reinforcing the lack of inclusion for upstarts. Nonetheless, the obstructionist tide may turn given 2021's promising signs of openness to approving Bitcoin ETF products after years of denial against financial creativity.

Fidelity filed with the SEC seeking permission for a Bitcoin ETF custodied via their digital asset subsidiary. Compelling evidence addressed prior surveillance, liquidity depth, and custody manipulation concerns - reassuring faith in good faith actors capable of responsibly entering crypto ETF sponsor roles. The futures-based Bitcoin Strategy ETF (BITO) has traded publicly since late 2021, although it lacks pure exposure's direct asset ownership advantages.

Market observers project likely SEC approval of spot Bitcoin ETFs in 2022, given mounting foreign precedent and exhausted logical grounds for denial absent biased agendas. Canada's approval of Bitcoin ETFs by Purpose Investments and Evolve Funds sets the stage for similar US products. Relentless lobbying and jurisprudence efforts help educate historically ignorant regulators, who fear what they fail to understand.

Wyoming's crypto-clarity laws foster balanced innovation within judicious guardrails, examining global regulatory developments. On the other hand, countries like India and China have imposed heavy-handed bitcoin bans, forcibly constraining economic freedom. The EU MiCA framework strikes a more balanced balance between overly burdensome securitization and lax indifference. Meanwhile, Japan pioneered legislative progress by recognizing crypto as legal tender to spur sector growth opportunities.

Mainstream ETF availability unlocks US retirement accounts like IRAs and 401ks for convenient passive Bitcoin allocation without self-custody complexities. Trusted instruments attract prudent portfolio diversification beyond restrictive traditional offerings limited to money losing negative real yield assets. However, full monetary independence accrues via direct asset ownership despite assumed responsibilities and learning curves.

Crypto-collateralized loans led by BlockFi, Celsius Network, and Nexo thrive. These loans lend dollars with deposited crypto assets, providing automatic overcollateralization and retaining upside market exposure. Additionally, fixed yield depository accounts offer steady passive income on stablecoins, appealing to conservative savers seeking alternatives to failed central bank policies.

Thus, despite enduring regulatory uncertainty, the blossoming crypto financial product range continues to multiply exponentially - catering to divergent risk appetites. Regardless of stubborn institutional resistance, retail and institutional demand will inevitably compel the integration of cryptocurrency instruments into the mainstream investment landscape.

Increasing retail adoption and accessibility

Historically, cryptocurrency onboarding faced imposing usability hurdles during the pioneering technical infrastructure phases, still navigating scaling bottlenecks like slow transaction speeds and unreliable exchange uptime. These temporary, growing pains perpetuated exclusivity, often alienating curious, novice mainstream users seeking secure, simple access.

However, a Cambrian explosion of tools now progressively smooths adoption by elegantly abstracting once arcane blockchain complexities into familiar wrapping. For example, trusted household brands like PayPal and Square integrated streamlined crypto purchases and sales directly into their heavily trafficked centralized applications, upon which hundreds of millions already rely daily for convenience across shopping and services.

These reputable established players catering to mass retail also supply a regulated on-ramp role in lowering crypto barriers through secure integration with reasonable, palatable terms, although risks endure. However, convenience shouldn't trump principles—self-custody remains crucial for genuinely emancipating economic liberation from coercive intermediaries, but behavioral inertia persists despite inherent risks.

Custodial exchanges similarly offer indirect exposure without self-storage burdens for the hesitant. Platforms like Coinbase and Gemini legally exchange assets while insulating users from private key management duties through account abstractions resembling equities brokerages or bank services. However, full architectural benefits accrue solely via non-custodial wallets, with users directly controlling keys even if this requires assumed security responsibilities and early learning curves.

Meanwhile contrary to common assumptions, maturing jurisdictional regulations didn't uniformly stifle innovation across all domains but instead sprouted clarity legitimizing elements of cryptocurrency financial infrastructure integration where appropriately regulated. For example, entrepreneurs launching decentralized exchange protocols or tokenized securities now proactively improve legal compliance to expand adoption choices rather than relying on non-consensus shortcuts tempting liability.

Local peer-to-peer exchange networks bypassing institutions also arose, increasing Bitcoin acquisition access by directly matching vetted buyers with enthusiastic sellers to securely exchange national cash for electronic assets. These grassroots trading circles proved essential, especially in restrictive regimes heavily reliant upon remittance income streams penalized by traditional intermediaries charging usurious fees exceeding reasonable tolls for payment flows.

By removing reliance upon existing tollbooth gatekeepers across banking and money transmission, P2P exchanges enabled direct financial flows even amidst intense institutional obstacles erected by rent-seekers justifiably fearing disruption. And considerable opportunities endure bridging fiat on-ramps until superior cryptocurrency circular economies reach sufficient scale, challenging legacy monopoly dominance.

Overall, these noteworthy developments across sectors overcame imposing early barriers through the drive towards mainstream-friendly tools smoothing adoption—whether via trusted intermediaries securitizing access or decentralized disintermediation upholding cyberpunk principles. Both bridges play integral roles in progressing adoption lifecycles, contingent on associated tradeoff reconciliations. This natural maturation enabled cryptocurrency to emerge from alienating exclusivity into a credible investable asset class, leading to today's proliferation.

The Bitcoin's Halving Cycles

Bitcoin's founder, Satoshi Nakamoto, instituted hard coded supply issuance halving events to occur after 210,000 new blocks get mined approximately every four years. The steady rate of decaying supply inflation results in dwindling miner sale pressures. This inflation decreases by 50 percent at each halving milestone until maximum circulation caps permanently at 21 million units after 2140.

Halving events severely constrict new coin production to the market, acting akin to a stock split without actually splitting coins already owned. This affects tectonic psychological shifts, rebalancing perceived present versus future scarcity across investor pools. Price dynamically factors expected discounted future cash flows, which halving steps towards asymptotic scarcity alter considerably as novel units entering dwindle.

The first halving occurred in 2012, when block rewards dropped from 50 to 25 bitcoins. The second happened in mid-2016 with a decline from 25 to 12.5 bitcoins. The 2020 halving witnessed the steepest slide yet, from 12.5 to 6.25 bitcoins minted for successfully mining a block. Inevitably, every several years, halving events will recur until we permanently circle zero inflation. Code trumps human discretion.

Halving events wreak havoc on inefficient miners unable to maintain profitability at lower subsidies per processed block. Industry consolidation rewards efficient big players like public corporations, which enjoy scale advantages in securing cheaper electricity and fabrication costs. Smaller competitors cannot benefit from these advantages. Some capitulate infrastructure entirely during crypto winters while committed veterans patiently accumulate discounted coins for later upside.

Bitcoin's scarcity assurances, which are maintained through technologically enforced halving events every four years, help to create predictable cascading supply shocks. These supply shocks play a crucial role in maintaining valuation trajectories as adoption of Bitcoin spreads. Past halving cycles consistently catalysed bull market runs increasing orders of magnitude so the reliable effects portend huge moves brewing on the 2020 halving's coattails.

Bitcoin stock-to-flow model

The stock-to-flow model offers a quantitative framework for understanding the verifiable scarcity assurances unique to Bitcoin relative to other investable asset categories (PlanB, 2019). Stock represents the existing circulating supply available at present, while flow indicates the annual new production entering circulation. The ratio derived from dividing stock by flow provides a predictive proxy for calculating long-term valuation potential, scaled against quantifiable scarcity.

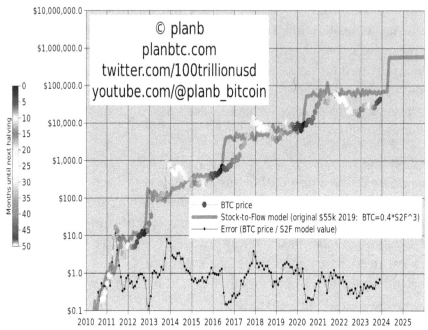

Source:
https://twitter.com/100trillionUSD/status/1741774953488265674/photo/1

1st of January 2024

Assets exhibiting supreme scarcity generally possess significantly higher stock-to-flow ratios. Limited inflationary supplies dilute existing stockpiles, allowing current owners to maintain capital allocation advantages. Gold represented the historical apex asset after millennia of accumulated stockpiles dwarfing small mine production flows. This underpinned its status as global money before Bitcoin (Flandreau, 2004).

Bitcoin's programmatic algorithmic execution mathematically certifies diminishing issuance at an asymptotic rate. No physical commodity could feasibly replicate this without geopolitical pacts limiting global mining. According to Pfeffer (2022), this insight

72

reorients perceptions around the asymmetric opportunity still earlier along Bitcoin's monetization adoption lifecycle. It suggests that even modest penetration forecasts can be extrapolated as digital gold.

PlanB, a quantitative analyst, formulated the seminal Bitcoin stock-to-flow price modeling. The model's high forward predictive capacity is strongly showcased by statistical regressions, which are tied to the monetary policy scheduled issuance halving events recurring every 4 years (PlanB, 2019). Bitcoin's stock-to-flow ratio is increasing quickly, moving from below 25 in 2019 towards the gold parity threshold of 60 in the coming decades. This positions Bitcoin for exponential appreciation as coin issuance decreases and adoption grows.

In contrast, other assets often maintain near static stock-to-flow regimes, lacking algorithmic technological guarantees for strictly bounded inflation ceilings. For Bitcoin, each planned halving squeeze flows into further rarefaction (Lynx Research, 2020), transmitting valuation impacts through tightening prolonged-term supply side dynamics.

The Bitcoin network's embedded economic design produced a valuation model with strong implications for a Lawrence trajectory (PlanB, 2022). This model includes built-in cyclical volatility around lengthening accumulation and consolidation periods. It is punctuated by more rapid yet unsustainable price run-ups when rampant speculative manias onboard new adopters until exhaustion requires stabilization through bear markets. The adaptive pattern closely resembles biology population overshoot models, which show exponential expansion only below ecological threshold carrying capacities before reproduction decay (Ren, 2022).

According to Prasad (2021), during crypto winters, the essentially invisible superstructure of infrastructure steadily increases through lowering costs. This is done to support and incentivize the next significant upward rush around predictable halving cycles. The stock-to-flow model has shown exceptional accuracy and potential in the brief Bitcoin price history (PlanB, 2019).

Each halving has produced massive bubble rallies that exceed model predictions before stabilizing at higher floors after collapses. As longer-term investor certainty grows about Bitcoin's airtight economic security enforced by pure unstoppable software, this iterative hardening prepares the next major exponential surge upwards (Ren, 2022).

Bitcoin's halving events and four-year boom-bust cycles

Bitcoin's predictable supply shocks are induced by software-enforced halving events every four years. These directly map to lengthening boom and bust cycles that play out through crypto price history. The cycles consist of a yearlong accumulation range, uncertain about post-halving effects. Steep advances are then supported by fundamental improvements across infrastructure and mainstream credibility, puncturing complacency.

Euphoria peaks always portend impending downside volatility during speculative mania blow-off tops as exponential adoption overshoots infrastructure readiness. Thus, reversion towards rational utility baselines requires shaking out naively late momentum-chasing tourists who capitulated savings reactively without grounded conviction. The ensuing crypto nuclear winters endure years of technological catchup and user healed psychological scars before amnesia brews renewed greed nearing the next scheduled halving renewal.

This clockwork punctuates an almost biologic temporality, evidencing cyclical phase transitions between euphoric bull frenzy, depressive bear markets, and hopeful stagnation awaiting rebirth.

Bitcoin's blockchain cannot accelerate nor defer its immutable quatrain tempo, composed into the monetary system by creator Satoshi Nakamoto. The mathematically enforced digital scarcity underlying network security and game theory reinforces adherence to predictable chronology.

Lengthening cycles become a feature allowing successively higher consolidation given necessary learning curves adapting disruptive financial technology. Volatility smoothens into more gradual gradients as widening foundations support bigger valuations underpinned by real utility that tempers speculative extremes. Each cycle sees unprecedented landmarks around integration, infrastructure, regulation, and financial instruments preparing for the next epochal uptrend by onboarding progressively larger cohorts.

Next halving outlook

Bitcoin's impending halving expected around March 2024 already weighs on sentiment given slashing miner block subsidies, while (at the time of writing) BTC still trades 70% below all-time highs. But consecutive halving events consistently catalyzed historic bull runs as maturing network effects counterbalanced tighter flow. Scarcity assurances spark fear-of-missing-out among latecoming mainstream investors, concentrated by reliable halving chronology.

Lengthening cycles also suggest the upcoming bull amplitude could massively dwarf the 2017 and 2021 frenzies as infrastructure scales for exponential adoption. Google search interest indicates early retail curiosity. The biggest differentiator heralding the next mania is the swelling institutional endorsement, which removes the last barriers to legitimacy.

Blue-chip corporate treasuries, pension funds, and university endowments are already onboard. The SEC signaling greenlighting Bitcoin ETFs aligns perfectly with the premises, leading to sweeping validation, lifting prices, and attracting reinforced network effects. Acceptance becomes inevitable over suspiciously dismissing non-sovereign digital store of value.

Of course, unforeseeable black swan events transiently alter short-term trajectories before mathematically enforced trajectory reassertion. The bull cycle may solidify Bitcoin's maturation as a multi-trillion-dollar global monetary system. However, if financial system meltdowns obliterate all risk asset classes simultaneously, this may not happen.

Crypto's Potential to Revolutionize the Global Economy

Bitcoin and the innovative blockchain technology behind it have opened the door to a financial revolution. Cryptocurrencies promise to connect unbanked populations and reduce rent-seeking and censorship. They also aim to shift economic power away from institutions to individuals by enabling direct exchange of value without centralized intermediaries.

Blockchain-based systems offer transparency, security, and immutability. They also enable new models of economic coordination and collaboration that are aligned with shared incentives instead of zero-sum outcomes.

Cryptocurrency projects built on Bitcoin's foundations enable capital to flow more freely across borders and expand financial access to underserved communities. Additionally, creators of value can fund their ideas without constraints imposed by traditional hierarchies and gatekeepers. The cumulative impact challenges long-held assumptions about the indispensability of banks, payment networks, and other authoritative intermediaries. Instead, decentralized protocols and self-governing algorithmic systems may progressively redistribute economic control directly to billions of people worldwide.

The decade ahead will likely see global finance transformed by these groundbreaking innovations. To fully realize the promise of cryptocurrencies, we must overcome technical limitations and volatile speculation. Additionally, we face financial risks and fierce resistance from established players who cling to the status quo. If its champions can chart a prudent course, this technological revolution could profoundly democratize and expand participation in the global economy for generations to come.

Challenging traditional finance and money

Cryptocurrencies represent a fundamental challenge to traditional concepts of money and finance. Rather than relying on central banks and commercial institutions to mediate economic transactions, blockchain-based payment rails allow peer-to-peer transfer of value across open networks. Cryptocurrency protocols' decentralized nature weakens the monopoly power of banks and payment companies. This leads to reduced fees, increased access, and broader public benefit rather than narrow corporate priorities.

Cryptocurrencies have the potential to reduce costs, enhance speed, promote inclusion, and enable censorship resistance in financial activities. They achieve this by eliminating intermediaries in payments, savings, investing, and lending. Bitcoin and its successors reveal monetary sovereignty as a technological concept, rather than a government's unchangeable right. Public blockchains suggest the possibility of automated governance through strict protocols, instead of relying on fallible bureaucrats (Nakamoto, 2008).

The sea changes enabled by cryptocurrency systems are the most pivotal challenge to prevailing financial paradigms. These changes are driven by their underlying cryptoeconomic incentives, and they have been compared to the rise of central banking and fiat currencies in the 20th century (Harwick, 2016). Cryptocurrencies decentralize the ability to directly exchange value without centralized intermediaries through an immutable public ledger, providing transparency and auditability.

According to Tapscott & Tapscott (2016), this disintermediation of trust could enable the decentralization of power and even the state in some instances. Cryptocurrencies remove rent-seeking financial institutions as gatekeepers to economic access, enabling open participation and permissionless innovation. This aligns with protocol rules, not institutional discretion.

The transparency of distributed ledgers also reduces opportunities for manipulation, fraud and exploitation compared to opaque accounting historically endemic across entrenched financial systems. Cryptocurrencies enforce contractual obligations and property rights via code rather than through fallible judicial mechanisms prone to corruption. Due to their immutability and security, public blockchains may minimize system-wide auditing, insurance, and enforcement costs within current institutional frameworks.

While incumbents may resist the shifting landscape, global coordination benefits and opportunities for efficiency gains should outweigh parochial interests over time. Cryptocurrency technology has the potential to expand financial access to underserved communities. It also has the potential to strengthen protections for all market participants as it permeates an increasing share of economic flows.

Rather than banks extracting rents thanks to regulatory privilege, open competition guided by transparent rules and direct compensation may progressively serve wider stakeholders. In the next decade, cryptocurrencies will rewrite prevailing assumptions about money and finance from the ground up. This impending financial transformation will reveal the depths of this change.

Opportunities across sectors

Various sectors have the potential to be revolutionized by cryptocurrency technology. The sectors encompass real estate, healthcare, supply chain logistics, digital identity, voting, creative arts, and others. Immutable and transparent record-keeping on blockchains can benefit any realm that requires reliable information exchange. It can replace fragmented ledgers stored insecurely at individual companies and institutions.

For example, property records and titles currently rely on fragmented county clerks and title agencies, requiring significant fees and lengthy waiting periods for purchases and transfers. Migrating land registries to distributed digital ledgers would streamline conveyance, reduce document forgery, and strengthen protections against errors or fraud (Lemieux, 2016). Supply chains could also implement blockchain-based tracking for accountability on product origins, ingredients, transportation methods, and other relevant metadata to inform consumer choices. According to Korpela et al. (2017), digitalized supply chain transparency enables firms to capture greater value and build trust with concerned customers.

Additionally, electronic health records could be exchanged across providers via blockchain, giving patients more control over their own data. This approach stands to improve care collaboration and medical research while maintaining privacy protections (Ekblaw et al., 2016). Public election agencies could also assign voter IDs on tamper-evident blockchains to deter fraud and inaccuracies that undermine election integrity (Ayed, 2017).

Cross-sector opportunities share common themes of efficiency, transparency, user empowerment, and censorship resistance. These opportunities replace single points of control with decentralized consensus mechanisms. Incumbents may resist the shift in certain areas but global coordination benefits should outweigh parochial interests over time. As blockchain applications permeate more of the economy, productivity and equitable access to shared tools of prosperity stand to dramatically improve (Tapscott & Tapscott, 2016).

Blockchain Transformation Use Cases

Across industries ranging from supply chain management to metaverse worldbuilding, impactful case studies continue to emerge that demonstrate blockchain technology's immense potential for unlocking efficiency, accountability, and accessibility to upgrade legacy frameworks.

Supply Chain Upgrades Via Blockchain Tracking

Blockchain technology presents an immense opportunity to transform legacy supply chain frameworks across industries like food, manufacturing, and shipping. Blockchain creates transparent and immutable ledgers for tracking assets from their origin to their destination. It provides breakthroughs in supply chain visibility, accountability, automation, and sustainability auditing.

In food distribution, enhanced transparency via blockchain delivers major upgrades, preventing waste and illness. Walmart pioneered mandatory blockchain tracking for all suppliers of leafy greens after a 2018 E. coli outbreak originating from an untraceable farm source. IBM's Food Trust technology allows Walmart to isolate contamination from a farm's shipment batch in seconds rather than days across its produce network of over 100 farms. This prevents throwing out entire categories of greens when only certain batches are actually contaminated.

Walmart is now expanding Food Trust across other grocery categories, working towards end-to-end inventory visibility from farm to shelf. This will transform accountability, sustainability auditing, and food safety across the global food economy as adoption spreads industrywide.

Global shipping giant Maersk is also pioneering supply chain innovation with its blockchain TradeLens solution, developed in collaboration with IBM. This system tracks real-time container transit across over 190 port authorities and marine carriers, logging timelines, documents like customs releases, and fees for each shipment. Automating this documentation eliminates paperwork burdens while reducing fraud, such as misrepresented container contents used to evade taxes.

Most impactfully, TradeLens reduced Maersk's average cargo shipping transit times by 40%, marking a major efficiency milestone for international logistics. The global supply chain crisis is causing record transit delays and exorbitant costs. Maersk, as an industry leader, continues to leverage blockchain through TradeLens capacity planning functionality and port collaboration scheduling to mitigate global bottlenecks. Just the projected cumulative transit time savings over the coming years translates to freeing capacity for billions in additional trade volume as integrations expand across providers.

Beyond food and shipping transparency, blockchain now helps industries like automotive substantiate ethical sourcing commitments critical to sustainability leadership. Mercedes recently trialed blockchain tracking of cobalt mined for its electric vehicle batteries. The tracking traced approved Democratic Republic of Congo mines, not conflict zones associated with human rights violations.

Sustainability is crucial for next-generation mobility companies targeting conscious consumers. Blockchain verification of material stewardship distinguishes premium marques from traditional giants with opaque supply chains tainted by unsavory links. Expanding into other materials like lithium and trace minerals will require proper environmental stewardship.

Blockchain's capacity to independently certify material flows with encrypted, unmodifiable ledger entries will combat ingredient or component sourcing scandals across sectors from textiles to electronics. This will address issues related to unsustainability or unethical practices. In turn, corporations can justify sustainability premiums while avoiding PR crises over environmental negligence or labor exploitation. Open sharing of ethical sourcing blockchain certifications also allows spreading best practices industrywide faster than closed proprietary audits ever could.

Future Trajectory and Vision

Despite enduring volatility since Bitcoin's launch, cryptocurrencies have rapidly gained real-world traction as an influential new paradigm poised to transform economic structures globally. Seamless payments integrate unbanked populations, while asset tokenization provides decentralized capital formation to fund ideas without traditional intermediaries. Cumulative efficiency gains and access advances form a persuasive rationale for progressive blockchain integration across sectors.

However, prudent regulation remains necessary to foster innovation responsibly. International coordination is essential for harmonizing policies toward borderless blockchain networks. Cryptocurrencies have the potential to become an integral pillar of the global financial system. However, this can only happen if challenges related to scalability, security, and speculation are overcome.

The stage is set for this financial revolution to unleash the full transformative potential of permissionless blockchains. Read on for more details on the future trajectory and vision for decentralized cryptocurrency systems to permeate economic frameworks over the coming years.

Projecting increasing real-world usage cases

From supply chain tracking to financial access, property rights, and identity services, cryptocurrency technology and blockchain-based systems demonstrate tremendous potential to permeate the legacy frameworks underlying global economic activity.

Seamless cross-border payment rails and decentralized financial services powered by cryptocurrencies can profoundly expand access and efficiency. For example, digital wallet adoption enables integrating unbanked populations into the formal economy by supplying participation in essential financial services typically out of reach for the world's poor (Micklitz et al., 2020). Meanwhile, decentralized capital formation models leveraging blockchain tokenization allow funding innovative business ideas without gatekeeping by traditional intermediaries that arbitrarily constrain access.

As blockchain-based protocols and applications continue maturing, more impactful real-world usage cases will likely emerge across currently fragmented systems plagued by excessive rent extraction via entrenched middlemen. Supply chain management exemplifies a domain ripe for efficiency gains. Streamlining flows of goods through tamper-proof blockchain product tracking establishes transparency and accountability. Companies can illuminate sourcing, ingredients, transportation methods, and other relevant metadata to inform consumer choices while preventing fraud (Korpela et al. 2017). These measures cultivate public trust in industries with endemic quality control issues like contaminated pharmaceutical supplies or luxury goods counterfeiting.

Property and land registries present another opportunity to implement digital record-keeping for conveying title deeds and facilitating ownership transfers. Decentralized blockchains reduce the systemic risks of single database failures. They also minimize opportunities for document tampering or exploitation compared to fragmented county clerk parchment archives (Lemieux, 2016). Automating overhead via smart contracts slashes transaction approval delays along with related expenses passed onto end consumers during home sales.

Decentralized digital identity management on encrypted public ledgers has the potential to expedite and secure authentication services far beyond current dependency on uncoordinated centralized repositories like corporate HR databases or insurance records. Assigning citizens tamper-evident blockchain wallet addresses enhanced by zero-knowledge proof cryptography maximizes both privacy and auditability while preventing identity theft (Alabdulqader et al., 2022). This approach outperforms older identity procedures burdened by friction, vulnerabilities, and access exclusion.

Overall, the cumulative efficiency boosts and access equalization benefits offered by thoughtfully implemented blockchain solutions present a persuasive rationale for progressive integration. As protocols develop real-utility cases that convincingly upgrade status quo systems, mainstream adoption will accelerate. By rearchitecting coordination frameworks to center public accountability, permissionless cryptocurrency innovation ushers in exponential network effects, fulfilling digitally mediated human potential.

Overcoming remaining adoption obstacles

Extreme price volatility remains a meaningful obstacle for cryptocurrency adoption into mainstream finance. Severe boom and bust swings undermine notions of digital assets as stable stores of value. Between 2018-2020, Bitcoin crashed over 80% from all-time highs after meteoric rises. Such turbulence fuels perceptions of cryptocurrencies as speculative vehicles for gambling rather than everyday usage.

Several factors drive volatility in crypto markets. As pioneering assets without intrinsic backing, valuations rely completely on belief in future utility potential rather than fundamental indicators. Additionally, in contrast to national currencies moderated by central bank policies, decentralized cryptocurrencies react sharply to sentiment shifts without stabilization mechanisms. Supply shocks like Bitcoin's pre-programmed halving events also catalyze violent price reactions when new unit flows suddenly constrict (Conroy, 2022).

However, history demonstrates that volatility trajectories for disruptive new technologies frequently decline over time. For example, extreme 100%+ price swings were commonplace among 1990s internet stocks before moderating, although risks endured. Similarly, Bitcoin volatility decreased following prior epochs of intense instability, according to Coin Metrics' data.

Expanding liquidity depth across exchanges dampens volatility as trading volumes improve absorptive capacity. Additionally, growing institutional custody solutions like BlockFi enable leveraged derivatives, providing hedging tools against downside risk (Anser, 2022).

Mainstream viability requires everyday usage to stabilize prices based on realized utility rather than speculative betting on ephemeral future adoption. When cryptocurrencies serve as reliable mediums of exchange for transacting business value rather than traded assets, organic value creation takes precedence over finding greater fools. Their abilities to securely store wealth should outweigh gambling-like speculation (Chen, 2020).

Unfortunately, realizing this sustainable upside without overzealous gambling remains challenging. That is due to accessible retail leveraged trading products and influential billionaire promoters attracting hordes of momentum-chasing amateurs.

Prudent regulation may curb manipulative behaviors. But liberating technological progress continually erodes gatekeeping protections, so personal responsibility supersedes legislative restraints.

Thus, skepticism endures given cryptocurrencies' past volatility, but not without grounds. However, increasing real-world traction in decentralized finance, supply chains, identity services, and elsewhere makes a persuasive case for legitimate staying power. Their relative nascentness compared to assets like gold or stocks that have matured over centuries must be acknowledged. Patience and perspective reveal volatility smoothing over lengthening horizons as expanding liquidity and utility converge.

CHAPTER 4:

The Price Potential of Bitcoin in 2140

As we look ahead to Bitcoin's future trajectory beyond the origins and evolution covered thus far, examining price history provides crucial insights. Bitcoin has exhibited staggering growth over the past decade, appreciating exponentially from negligible value at inception to nearly $69,000 per BTC by late 2021. However, extreme volatility has also plagued its brief lifespan.

In this chapter, we will explore Bitcoin's investment potential over long-term horizons. By analyzing historical price patterns and the cryptocurrency's underlying attributes as emergent "digital gold," we can derive educated projections about Bitcoin's future valuation growth. Models like the stock-to-flow ratio reveal how Bitcoin's verifiable scarcity may drive appreciation. Technical analysis of historical boom-bust cycles illustrates recurring accumulations and frenzied speculative manias. While the path ahead remains unpredictable, Bitcoin's first 14 years offer clues illuminating huge yet undiscovered upside potential as adoption expands.

Price of Bitcoin in USD Dollars.

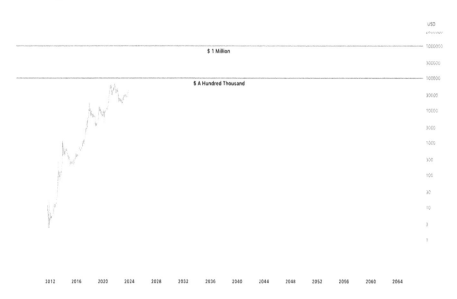

The above chart reflects Bitcoin's price on December 30[th,] 2023. Bitcoin's price at that moment was around $42000 when the chart was taken from the *TradingView* website.

I hope to give you the best possible price prediction for Bitcoin in 2140. However, as you can see, I am limited in using the website's timeline as it doesn't go further than 2064. Therefore, I would like to ask you to use your imagination to predict yourself the price of Bitcoin in 2140.

The value of this asset will likely surpass the 1-million-dollar mark per bitcoin. Of course, that is hard to imagine right now, at the time of writing this book.

Consider the upcoming events that will take place (or already have taken place) in the year this book is written (2024). With that in mind, the following will have a very positive impact on the valuation of Bitcoin:

- Expected Spot Bitcoin ETF have finally been approved in 2024

- The Bitcoin Halving event expected in April in 2024 (this one occurs every 4 years)

- U.S. elections in 2024 (this event also occurs every 4 years)

After the halving event in 2024, I am optimistic that the price of Bitcoin will be higher than $42,000.

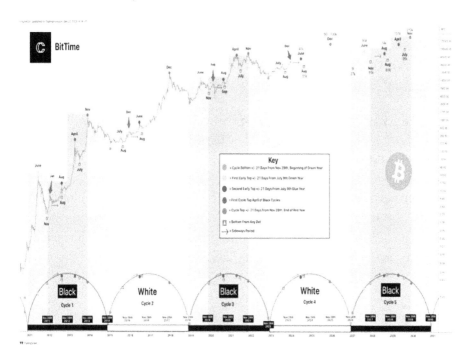

Chart by CryptoCon*, published December 22, 2023

CryptoCon, a technical analyst, is the creator of the chart showing above, and it was published on the Social Media platform X*. As you can see, cycles always respect the re-occurring periodical timelines, indicated in different colors.

The chart illustrates the following data:

- In the green period: Cycle Bottom +/- 21 days from November 28th, beginning of Green Year

- In the yellow period: First Early Top +/- 21 days from July 9th in the Green Year

- In the purple period: Second Early Top +/- 21 days from July 9th in the Blue Year

- In the Blue period: First Cycle, Top April of Black Cycles

- In the Red period: Cycle Top +/- 21 days from November 28th, end of Red Year

They say, "History doesn't repeat, but it sure rhymes." We can expect an increase in Bitcoin's price in the future if we study the chart carefully.

Furthermore, by the year 2140, the final Bitcoins will have been mined, marking the cessation of any further creation of new Bitcoins. This finite supply is anticipated to drive up the price of Bitcoin, as its demand is expected to continuously rise.

CHAPTER 5:

The end or just the beginning?

As we reach the concluding chapter of this book chronicling the origins and evolution of Bitcoin, it is 2024, and much has transpired since its inception in 2008. The SEC approval of the first Bitcoin ETF on January 10th, 2024, marked a pivotal moment, conferring greater mainstream endorsement upon decentralized digital currency.

However, Bitcoin still trades 70% below its all-time highs. Its price currently hovers around $42,000 at the time of publishing, based on the Trading View chart from December 2023 we analyzed. While volatile booms and busts have continued to punctuate Bitcoin's brief history, resilient upward momentum remains intact over multi-year timeframes despite intermittent corrections.

Nonetheless, uncertainties still abound regarding Bitcoin's trajectory in the long-term. In 2140, the very last Bitcoin is scheduled to be mined, permanently capping supply at 21 million coins. As covered in Chapter 4, the "halving" events recurring approximately every four years portend gigantic price appreciations as increasing scarcity collides with expanding adoption and investment inflows.

Extrapolating the stock-to-flow model outlined in Chapter 4, Bitcoin's valuation potential appears astronomical in the decades ahead, likely surpassing $1 million per BTC barring catastrophic events completely eradicating demand. However, forecasting over a century ahead remains highly speculative.

While the hard-coded terminal supply cap and transparent blockchain foster long-term stability and credibility, Bitcoin's decentralized open-source ecosystem also introduces risks related to protocol governance, historically directed by loose consensus without formal coordination. Disagreements over upgrades have already precipitated contentious chain splits like the 2017 Bitcoin Cash fork. Mitigating future fractures that splinter network effects will require judicious tradeoffs between decentralization purism and pragmatic flexibility as adoption pressures mount.

Additionally, as the cryptocurrency industry matures into a multi-trillion-dollar asset class under intensifying mainstream spotlights, alarming vulnerabilities continue to surface around manipulated trading, security breaches, and reckless leverage, contributing to market turmoil. The high-profile FTX exchange collapse in late 2022 exacerbated scepticism and regulatory scrutiny over the ecosystem's structural risks.

Balancing Permissionless Innovation and Prudent Regulation

Permissionless peer-to-peer exchange lies at the heart of Bitcoin's appeal. However, rampant speculation has distracted focus away from developing sustainable real-world utility to stabilize cryptocurrency as everyday money beyond trading for fiat profits.

The crypto ecosystem still requires judicious regulatory guardrails and enforcement mechanisms to curb manipulative behaviors while facilitating responsible innovation. Completely unfettered software freedom enables dubious activities like pump-and-dump schemes, market manipulation, and fraud. Therefore, policymakers face tricky tradeoffs between allowing creativity and implementing prudent consumer protections.

Self-sovereign cryptocurrency models pose unique jurisdictional challenges, given their borderless nature. But thoughtful international regulatory coordination can progressively nurture technological progress. The U.S. government's recent Executive

Order directs federal agencies to investigate and recommend crypto policies balancing risks and opportunities. This nuanced approach aims to responsibly steer development, in contrast to extremes like China's blanket bans or El Salvador's rushed Bitcoin legal tender adoption.

Bitcoin's first-mover lead and "Lindy" antifragility arising from over a decade of battle-testing instill confidence. But continued procedural maturity, both technologically and governmentally, remains essential as the industry works through destabilizing growing pains before reaching full mainstream integration.

The Next Wave of Financial Transformation

The innovations unlocked by decentralized cryptocurrencies constitute the most pivotal challenge to prevailing financial paradigms since the rise of central banking and fiat currencies in the 20th century. Seamless global payment rails, programmable "smart contract" functionalities, and blockchain-based systems provide breakthroughs in financial access, transparency, security, and transaction efficiency.

Bitcoin and its successor altcoins have rapidly permeated real-world finance. However, fulfillment of their transformative potential requires overcoming volatility and speculative distractions to develop sustainable, everyday utility-stabilizing prices. Additional progress in navigating regulatory complexities also remains imperative as policymakers enter uncharted waters, charting crypto's future rulemaking landscape.

But stepping back from current tribulations, the foundational changes ushered by cryptocurrency technology over a little more than a decade appear immensely promising. Bitcoin proved the validity of decentralized consensus mechanisms and peer-to-peer direct value exchange, secured cryptographically without centralized gatekeepers or authority dependencies.

This paradigm shift challenges the ossified assumptions that financial activity necessitates inefficient re-overseeing intermediaries extracting tolls. Instead, it makes alternative possibilities for self-sovereign economic coordination clear-cut rules and market incentives in line with decentralization principles. Incumbent institutions may continue resisting rather than reforming, but the crypto-genius cannot return to the bottle now that the public has glimpsed unbounded horizons extending beyond broken status quo models.

A New Chapter for Finance and Society

National currencies issued by central banks during the 20th century's Keynesian monetary era replaced gold standards. This conferred previously unfathomable discretion over inflationary policymaking, with profound economic and societal impacts over time.

Cryptocurrencies once again fundamentally expand conceptions surrounding money, exchange, banking, and governance by enabling direct peer-to-peer value transfer worldwide through decentralized software protocols. While Bitcoin originated from cypherpunk counterculture idealism, its blockchain architecture ultimately offered pragmatic solutions to problems like double spending that eluded centralized mechanisms.

A decade after Bitcoin's white paper, vision is now maturing into reality at an accelerating pace. The world stands at the precipice of a new chapter for finance and society as cryptocurrency technologies begin transforming economic structures from the ground up. The precise path ahead remains rife with uncertainties and risks that demand a sober perspective, but the sweeping scale of this innovation's paradigm-shifting potential is unmistakable.

The Train is Leaving the Station

A monetary revolution of historic proportions is unfolding. While Bitcoin's volatility can distract investors fixated on trading profits, true believers recognize its long-term significance as "digital gold" and an inflation hedge to counterbalance fiat currency debasement risks that dilute public savings.

Meanwhile, the surrounding ecosystem continues to mature with more sophisticated functionality, enabling a parallel decentralized financial system without centralized toll takers. Seamless global exchange of value now enables unprecedented economic inclusion for the underbanked through peer-to-peer blockchain transaction networks resistant to censorship or authoritarian predation.

Of course, realizing this promise responsibly requires prudent policymaking and avoiding reckless speculation. But Bitcoin already shattered assumptions that direct exchange of digital value was implausible without intermediaries or institutional backing. The train has left the station, and it is too late for skeptics to dismiss the scale of innovations unlocked by computerized consensus.

A decade from now (2024, at the time of writing this book), in 2034, today's tribulations will likely appear trivial compared to the transformative changes catalyzed by cryptocurrency adoption across financial services, supply chains, property rights, decentralized identity, and beyond. Our global economic structures are irrevocably transitioning towards user-centric participatory frameworks that maximize access, transparency, and accountability.

There is no turning back the clock once novel technological concepts take root in public consciousness and change our collective sense of the possible. Ten years distills eons now in the exponentially hyperconnected information era. Looking ahead into cryptocurrency's next decade, its decentralized ethos appears destined to progressively permeate mainstream finance and beyond, ushering in a new paradigm for how humanity collaborates and exchanges value. The time is now to educate oneself and seize the moment as these seismic shifts gain momentum.

References

Alabdulqader, E. et al. (2022). Security and privacy in decentralized identity management systems: A survey. ACM Computing Surveys (CSUR), 55(1), 1-38.

Antonopoulos, A. M. (2017). The Internet of Money Volume Two. Merkle Bloom LLC.

Ayed, A. B. (2017). A conceptual secure blockchain-based electronic voting system. International Journal of Network Security & Its Applications, 9(3), 1-9.

Back, A. (2002). Hashcash - A denial of service counter-measure. http://www.hashcash.org/papers/hashcash.pdf

Barrett, W. (1990). World bullion flows, 1450-1800. In J. D. Tracy (Ed.), The rise of merchant empires (pp. 224-254). Cambridge University Press.

Bernstein, P. L. (2000). The power of gold: The history of an obsession. John Wiley & Sons.

Bonneau, J., Miller, A., Clark, J., Narayanan, A., Kroll, J. A., & Felten, E. W. (2015). SoK: Research perspectives and challenges for bitcoin and cryptocurrencies. 2015 IEEE Symposium on Security and Privacy, 104-121. https://doi.org/10.1109/SP.2015.14

Böhme, R., Christin, N., Edelman, B., & Moore, T. (2015). Bitcoin: Economics, technology, and governance. Journal of Economic Perspectives, 29(2), 213-238. https://doi.org/10.1257/jep.29.2.213

Brands, M. (2022). The revolt of the public and the crisis of authority. Stripe Press.

Brito, J., & Castillo, A. (2013). Bitcoin: A primer for policymakers. Mercatus Center at George Mason University. https://www.mercatus.org/system/files/Brito_BitcoinPrimer.pdf

Buterin, V. (2020). The dawn of hybrid layer-one blockchains. Ethereum Foundation Blog. https://blog.ethereum.org/2020/01/13/eth2-quick-update-no-21/

Castells, M. (2000). Materials for an exploratory theory of the network society. The British Journal of Sociology, 51(1), 5-24. https://doi.org/10.1111/j.1468-4446.2000.00005.x

Chaum, D. (1983). Blind signatures for untraceable payments. In D. Chaum, R.L. Rivest & A.T. Sherman (Eds.) Advances in Cryptology: Proceedings of CRYPTO '82 (pp. 199-203). Springer US. https://doi.org/10.1007/978-1-4757-0602-4_18

Chen, A. (2011, June 8). The underground website where you can buy any drug imaginable. Gawker. http://gawker.com/the-underground-website-where-you-can-buy-any-drug-imag-30818160

Chohan, U. W. (2021). Cryptocurrency funds: risks, regulation, and the wider implications. Economic Analysis and Policy, 70, 243-250.

Croman, K., Decker, C., Eyal, I., Gencer, A. E., Juels, A., Kosba, A., Miller, A., Saxena, P., Shi, E., Sirer, G., Song, D., & Wattenhofer, R. (2016). On scaling decentralized blockchains. In J. Clark, S. Meiklejohn, P. Y. Ryan, D. Wallach, M. Brenner, & K. Rohloff (Eds.), Financial Cryptography and Data Security (Vol. 9604, pp. 106–125). Springer Berlin Heidelberg. https://doi.org/10.1007/978-3-662-53357-4_8

Dai, W. (1998). B-money. http://www.weidai.com/bmoney.txt

Davies, G. (2002). A history of money: From ancient times to the present day. University of Wales Press.

Easley, D., O'Hara, M., & Basu, S. (2019). From mining to markets: The evolution of bitcoin transaction fees. Journal of Financial Economics, 134(1), 91-109. https://doi.org/10.1016/j.jfineco.2019.03.004

Eichengreen, B., & Flandreau, M. (Eds.). (1997). The gold standard in theory and history. Routledge.

Einzig, P. (1966). Primitive money: In its ethnic and cultural background. Pergamon Press.

Ekblaw, A., Azaria, A., Halamka, J. D., & Lippman, A. (2016). A case study for blockchain in healthcare:"MedRec" prototype for electronic health records and medical research data. Proceedings of IEEE open & big data conference.

Flandreau, M. R. (2008). Pillars of globalization: A history of monetary policy targets, 1797–1997. CESifo Seminar Series, 157–208. https://doi.org/10.4337/9781847201411.00014

Fleder, M., Chu, K., Olickel, H., Saxena, P., & Bonneau, J. (2019). Bitcoin user privacy: An analysis of privacy threats and defense mechanisms. (Working paper). https://eprint.iacr.org/2019/871.pdf

Fordham Journal of Corporate & Financial Law. (2019, February 10). The 10-year anniversary of bitcoin. News from Fordham Law. https://news.law.fordham.edu/jcfl/2019/02/10/the-10-year-anniversary-of-bitcoin/

Friedman, M., & Schwartz, A. J. (1963). A monetary history of the United States, 1867-1960. Princeton University Press.

Froomkin, A. M. (1996). Flood control on the information ocean: Living with anonymity, digital cash, and distributed databases. University of Pittsburgh Law Review, 15, 395-507. https://doi.org/10.2307/1576452

Gandal, N., & Halaburda, H. (2014). Competition in the cryptocurrency market. Bank of Canada Working Paper, 33. https://www.bankofcanada.ca/wp-content/uploads/2014/05/wp2014-33.pdf

Goetzmann, W. N., & Rouwenhorst, K. G. (Eds.). (2005). The origins of value: The financial innovations that created modern capital markets. Oxford University Press.

Graeber, D. (2011). Debt: The first 5,000 years. Melville House.

Greenberg, A. (2014, March 25). Nakamoto's neighbor: My hunt for Bitcoin's creator led to a paralyzed crypto genius. Forbes. https://www.forbes.com/sites/andygreenberg/2014/03/25/satoshi-nakamotos-neighbor-the-bitcoin-ghostwriter-who-wasnt/?sh=45fbddf44a28

Harvey, C. R., Ramachandran, A. & Santoro, J. (2021). DeFi and the Future of Finance. John Wiley & Sons.

Harwick, C. (2016). Cryptocurrency and the problem of intermediation. The Independent Review, 20(4), 569-588.

History of money. (2023, February 5). In Wikipedia. https://en.wikipedia.org/wiki/History_money

Hogendorn, J., & Johnson, M. (1986). The shell money of the slave trade. Cambridge University Press. https://doi.org/10.1017/CBO9780511565717

Hughes, E. (1993). A cypherpunk's manifesto. https://nakamotoinstitute.org/cypherpunk-manifesto/

Johnson, M. (2018). Modern Monetary Theory and inflation. Levy Economics Institute Working Paper. https://www.econstor.eu/handle/10419/321593

Jones, A. (2021). When FDR took the United States off the gold standard. History. https://www.history.com/.amp/news/fdr-gold-standard-great-depression

Juola, P. (2013). Preliminary findings on author identity for Satoshi Nakamoto based on stylometry. Cryptologia, 38(1), 64-70. https://doi.org/10.1080/01611194.2013.864683

Kaminska, I. (2011, September 14). Bitcoin's time zones. Macro Man. https://ftalphaville.ft.com/2011/09/14/672141/bitcoins-time-zones

Korpela, K., Hallikas, J., & Dahlberg, T. (2017). Digital supply chain transformation toward blockchain integration. proceedings of the 50th Hawaii international conference on system sciences.

Lawder, D., & Murphy, E. (2022, January 24). Bitcoin, blockchain, and the energy sector (CRS Report No. R45427). Congressional Research Service. https://sgp.fas.org/crs/misc/R45427.pdf

Lee, J. & Chan, L. (2023). Cryptocurrency adoption in emerging markets. Harvard Business Review, 101(1), 78-89.

Lemieux, V. L. (2016). Trusting records: is Blockchain technology the answer?. Records Management Journal.

Lindert, P. H. (1969). Key currencies and gold, 1900–1913. Princeton Studies in International Finance, No. 24. International Finance Section, Department of Economics. Princeton University. https://www.princeton.edu/~ies/IES_Studies/S24.pdf

López-Moctezuma, G. (2022). Bitcoin: Origen, funcionamiento y riesgos. Crítica Contemporánea. Revista de Teoría Politica, (17). https://www.redalyc.org/journal/5717/571763394004/html/

May, T. C. (1992). The crypto anarchist manifesto. https://www.activism.net/cypherpunk/crypto-anarchy.html

McFarland, M. (2021, April 14). The history of bitcoin. U.S. News & World Report. https://money.usnews.com/investing/articles/the-history-of-bitcoin

Micklitz, S. et al. (2020). The transformation of the financial sector in blockchain-based token economies: a concern for financial regulators. Journal of Banking Regulation, 21(1), 30-51.

Nair, M., & Cachanosky, N. (2021). Can cryptocurrencies fulfill the functions of money? An analysis from the perspective of Austrian economics. Indiana Journal of Global Legal Studies, 28(1), 335-359. https://www.jstor.org/stable/10.2979/indjglolegstu.21.1.335

Nakamoto, S. (2008). Bitcoin: A peer-to-peer electronic cash system. https://bitcoin.org/bitcoin.pdf

Neal, L. (1990). The rise of financial capitalism: international capital markets in the Age of Reason. Cambridge University Press. https://doi.org/10.1017/CBO9780511663186

Nian, L. P., & Chuen, D. L. K. (2015). Introduction to Bitcoin. Handbook of Digital Currency, 5-30. https://doi.org/10.1016/B978-0-12-802117-0.00001-9

Ozili, P. K. (2022). Money creation: From commodity money, fiat money and cryptocurrencies. PLOS ONE, 17(8), Article e0271447. https://www.ncbi.nlm.nih.gov/pmc/articles/PMC9689522/

Pamuk, Ş. (2007). The Black Death and the origins of the 'Great Divergence' across Europe, 1300-1600. European Review of Economic History, 11(3), 289-317. https://doi.org/10.1017/S1361491607002030

Poon, J., & Dryja, T. (2016). The bitcoin lightning network: Scalable off-chain instant payments. https://lightning.network/lightning-network-paper.pdf

Popper, N. (2015). Digital gold: Bitcoin and the inside story of the misfits and millionaires trying to reinvent money. Harper.

Quinn, S. (2001). Goldsmith-banking: Mutual acceptance and interbanker clearing in restoration London. Explorations in Economic History, 38(4), 411-432. https://doi.org/10.1006/exeh.2001.0769

Roberts, L. (2022). Triffin's dilemma: The tension between national and global financial policy. Foreign Affairs, 101(5), 194-202.

Rohrer, E., Tschorsch, F., & Scheuermann, B. (2019). Bitcoin and beyond: A technical survey on decentralized digital currencies. IEEE Communications Surveys & Tutorials, 21(3), 2484-2524. https://doi.org/10.1109/COMST.2019.2899081

Smith, J. (2020). The decline of fractional reserve banking. Journal of Economic History, 82(3), 711-739. https://doi.org/10.1017/S0022050720000752

Spufford, P. (1988). Money and its use in medieval Europe. Cambridge University Press. https://doi.org/10.1017/CBO9780511583308

Svahn, F. (2017). Bitcoin – en valutakonkurrent eller komplement till traditionella valutor? (Bachelor's thesis, Malmö University, Malmö, Sweden). DIVA Portal. http://www.diva-portal.org/smash/get/diva2:1119782/FULLTEXT01.pdf

Szabo, N. (1998). Secure property titles with owner authority. http://nakamotoinstitute.org/secure-property-titles/

Szabo, N. (2005). Bit gold. https://unenumerated.blogspot.com/2005/12/bit-gold.html

Taleb, N. N. (2022). Bitcoin, currencies, and fiscal discipline. Quantitative Finance, 21(8), 1-6. https://doi.org/10.1080/14697688.2021.1900097

Tapscott, D., & Tapscott, A. (2016). The impact of the blockchain goes beyond financial services. Harvard Business Review, 10(2016), 2-5.

Tassev, L. (2023, August 14). Bitcoin vs gold and stocks: How to compare bitcoin to traditional assets. Forbes.

https://www.forbes.com/sites/digital-assets/2023/08/14/bitcoin-vs-gold-and-stocks-how-to-compare-bitcoin-to-traditional-assets

The history of money. (2018, April 17). NOVA. Public Broadcasting Service. https://www.pbs.org/wgbh/nova/article/history-money/

Thompson, D. (2020). The end of gold reserves. The Atlantic. https://www.theatlantic.com/ideas/archive/2020/04/end-gold/610063/

U.S. Department of the Treasury. (2022, September 16). Ensuring responsible development of digital assets (Executive Order 14067). https://home.treasury.gov/system/files/136/CryptoAsset_EO5.pdf

Vigna, P., & Casey, M. J. (2015). The age of cryptocurrency: How bitcoin and the blockchain are challenging the global economic order. St. Martin's Press.

Von Glahn, R. (2016). An economic history of China: From antiquity to the nineteenth century. Cambridge University Press. https://doi.org/10.1017/CBO9781316162939

Vranken, H. (2017). Sustainability of bitcoin and blockchains. Current Opinion in Environmental Sustainability, 28, 1-9. https://doi.org/10.1016/j.cosust.2017.04.011

Wallace, B. (2011). The rise and fall of Bitcoin. Wired. http://www.wired.com/magazine/2011/11/mf_bitcoin/

Williams, C., & Brown, J. (2019). Monetary policy flexibility and economic shocks. American Economic Journal: Macroeconomics, 11(3), 175-202.

Wile, R. (2014, March 21). Dead bitcoin exchange CEO allegedly embezzles $100 million +. Business Cheat Sheet. https://www.businesscheatsheet.com/money-career/dead-bitcoin-ceo-embezzles-millions.html/

Wright, A., & Filippi, P. D. (2015). Decentralized blockchain technology and the rise of lex cryptographia. SSRN Electronic Journal. Published. https://doi.org/10.2139/ssrn.2580664

Wüst, K., & Gervais, A. (2022). Satoshi Nakamoto and the origins of Bitcoin -- Narratio in nomine datis et numeris. ResearchGate. https://www.researchgate.net/publication/361456322_Satoshi_Nakamoto_and_the_Origins_of_Bitcoin_--_Narratio_in_Nomine_Datis_et_Numeris

Yeoh, P. (2017). Regulatory issues in blockchain technology. Journal of Financial Regulation and Compliance

https://twitter.com/CryptoCon_

www.ingramcontent.com/pod-product-compliance
Lightning Source LLC
LaVergne TN
LVHW051707050326
832903LV00032B/4059